From Your Friends at **The MAILBOX®**

# Short Short Stories
## FOR READING ALOUD

# Grade 5
## *Table of Contents*

# How to Use This Book

Stretch your readers to higher levels with short short read-alouds that expand listening comprehension abilities, build vocabulary, and foster a lifelong love of reading. Each story in this collection—both fiction and creative nonfiction—has been carefully selected to provide high-interest, age- and grade-appropriate material that will grab your students' attention. Each story can be read in ten minutes or less, making it easy to include purposeful story sharing in your busy day. Organized by genre, these stories introduce students to a wide range of texts from a variety of cultures and time periods. You'll find everything from humor to realistic. Read aloud, and enjoy!

**Why Read Aloud?**

Reading aloud at a level above students' reading comprehension level increases listening comprehension, an essential skill for understanding texts and success in reading. In addition, reading aloud provides a model of fluent reading, develops a sense of story, expands vocabulary, promotes good grammar, and encourages active and appreciative listening. The 50 original short short stories in this book will open your students' eyes to people, places, and things that are just beyond their ability to read and understand on their own.

**Preparing Students to Listen**

Reading these stories aloud to your students will certainly help develop listening skills as well as expand vocabulary. But *preparing* students to listen helps them become *more effective* listeners.

*Discuss the purpose for listening.*

For example, while listening to these short short stories, students may listen for information, listen for pleasure, or listen to empathize.

*Activate prior knowledge.*

Discuss backgrounds, experiences, beliefs, attitudes, or biases that may affect the listening experience.

*Invite students to make predictions.*

Use the story's title, genre, or illustration to involve students in a discussion of what might happen in the story.

*Identify and discuss vocabulary.*

Identify vocabulary words in the story and then have students predict possible meanings. After reading, check students' predictions.

## Aiding Comprehension

Guide students through the listening process and ensure comprehension using one or more of the following strategies.

*Stop and summarize.*

Plan to stop after important events and ask students to summarize what has happened so far, review previous predictions, or make predictions about what might happen next.

*Invite inferences.*

Have students listen for meaning between the lines. For example, after reading about a character's actions, appearance, or surroundings, ask students to make inferences about the character's personality.

*Encourage guided imagery.*

Have students form pictures in their heads to go along with the story.

*Promote thoughtful inquiry.*

Have students jot down vocabulary words, interesting facts, or questions while they listen.

## Assessing Comprehension

The Comprehension Check at the end of each story offers a quick way to assess comprehension. Questions may be asked during the reading, since they are chronological in order, or after the reading (either orally or in writing). Answer keys are provided on pages 109–112.

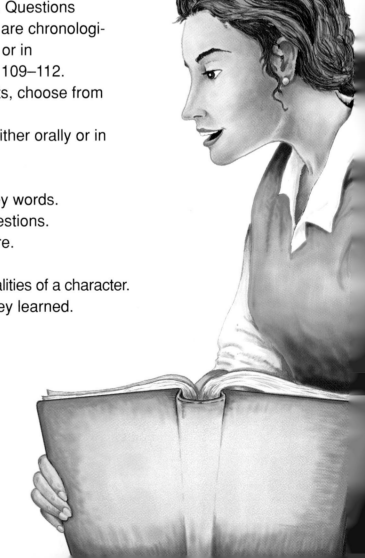

For additional quick and easy assessments, choose from the following:

- Ask students to summarize the story (either orally or in writing).
- Ask students to illustrate the story.
- Ask students to identify meanings of key words.
- Ask students to formulate their own questions.
- Ask students to identify the story's genre.
- Ask students to list significant details.
- Ask students to write down three key qualities of a character.
- Ask students to list three new things they learned.

Read aloud and enjoy these short short stories often to give students plenty of listening practice!

**From Your Friends at The MAILBOX®**

# Short Short Stories
## FOR READING ALOUD

**Project Editors:** Kim T. Griswell, Cayce Guiliano
**Copy Editors:** Gina Farago, Karen Brewer Grossman, Karen L. Huffman, Amy Kirtley, Debbie Shoffner
**Cover Artist:** Clevell Harris
**Art Coordinator:** Mary Lester
**Artists:** Pam Crane, Teresa Davidson, Theresa Lewis Goode, Nick Greenwood, Sheila Krill, Mary Lester, Clint Moore, Kimberly Richard, Greg D. Rieves, Barry Slate, Donna K. Teal
**Typesetters:** Lynette Maxwell, Mark Rainey

**President, The Mailbox Book Company™:** Joseph C. Bucci
**Book Development Managers:** Stephen Levy, Elizabeth H. Lindsay, Thad McLaurin, Susan Walker
**Book Planning Manager:** Chris Poindexter
**Curriculum Director:** Karen P. Shelton
**Traffic Manager:** Lisa K. Pitts
**Librarian:** Dorothy C. McKinney
**Editorial and Freelance Management:** Karen A. Brudnak
**Editorial Training:** Irving P. Crump
**Editorial Assistants:** Terrie Head, Melissa B. Montanez, Hope Rodgers, Jan E. Witcher

## www.themailbox.com

# Dinner at Dave's House

*by Karen Cogan*

Dave stood in front of the tomato vines he had grown, feeling rather perplexed. He was proud of these tomatoes. They were red and shiny and ready to be picked, but Dave had a problem—his family was about to move. He wasn't about to abandon his crop by leaving the tomatoes behind when he moved to his new house. It was bad enough that he had to leave the neighborhood he'd lived in his whole life. It was worse that he had to leave his friends behind. He wasn't going to leave his tomatoes behind. There had to be a way to carry them without smashing them.

Rummaging through the odds and ends his mom had left in the garage to be discarded, Dave found an empty box labeled "worms." His mom had ordered the worms to aerate the soil last spring. The wiggly worms dug tunnels in the earth, creating a complicated maze of burrows that allowed the soil to breathe. The box they had arrived in was just the right size.

Dave picked the tomatoes, put them in the box, and then crumpled packing paper and stuffed it between the tomatoes to provide protection. Finally, he taped the box shut.

Back in the garage, Dave examined the piles of boxes packed and ready for the moving company. He hesitated before adding his box to the stack. He didn't want it to get mixed up with those; it might take weeks to unearth his tomatoes in the new garage. By then, he was sure they would be inedible. No one would want to eat tomatoes covered with the weird, furry growth that would probably cover them by the time he found them. So Dave stowed his special box in the car.

That afternoon, Dave's family piled into the car. Dave hugged his box against his chest as they turned the corner, leaving his old neighborhood behind. When they reached the new house, Dave struggled out of the car with the sealed box. As he straightened up, he noticed a boy watching from across the street. The boy walked over.

"I'm Frank," he said. "I live over there." He pointed to his house.

"I'm Dave. We're moving in. Want to help me get this box inside?" Dave nodded at the cardboard box with the word *worms* printed on it.

Frank looked at the box. He read the label and shrugged nonchalantly.

"Sure, I guess so. Why is it taped? So they won't get out?"

"No," Dave replied. "I just wanted to protect them. I didn't trust the moving van with these. I planted them myself."

"You planted them?"

"Yeah. I'm going to put them in the refrigerator until Mom can cook them."

"Cook them?" Frank gave Dave a funny look.

Dave nodded. "They make good spaghetti sauce."

"Where are you from?" Frank asked. "Outer space?"

Dave paused. "No. Jonestown."

"You eat those there?"

"Sure. The big ones are really juicy. What do you do with them?"

"I take them fishing with me."

Dave looked at Frank. "Why? Do you put them on your sandwich?"

Frank wrinkled his nose in disgust. "Yuck!"

"Say, Mom's boiling some for supper. Why don't you come by and try them?"

"Thanks, but I think we're having meat loaf." Frank backed hastily away.

Dave opened his box and carefully set his tomatoes on the counter. Frank was a strange kid. If they became friends, he'd have to remember how much Frank hated tomatoes.

##  Comprehension Check

**1.** Why is Dave so protective of the tomatoes?

**2.** How do you think Dave feels about moving? Why?

**3.** What makes this story funny?

**4.** Do you think that Dave and Frank will become friends? Why or why not?

# Whac-A-Mole®!

*by Kim T. Griswell*

The only thing that Cody would have liked better than spending an afternoon in the arcade with five bucks in his pocket was doing it without his pesky little sister, Emily. His folks thought Emily was some kind of blue-eyed, blond-haired angel, but Cody thought differently. He was sure she was an alien sent down from a mother ship on the dark side of the moon for the sole purpose of bugging him. Obviously, the aliens wanted to see just how much an 11-year-old Earth boy could take before he cracked.

As always, he checked out the prizes in the glass cases before he started accumulating tickets. The arcade back home had great prizes: *Star Wars* mugs, stink bombs, fuzzy dice…. This one had things like Minnie® Mouse statuettes and mirrors framed in fake fur. Cody was about to back away in dismay when he spotted a velvet basset hound. A heavy sensation settled in his chest. Then it kind of twisted around like a boa, tightening until his lungs let out a heavy sigh.

"I know how much you love George," his mom had said. "But we can't drive 3,500 miles in a moving van with him sitting on our laps. It wouldn't be fair to him or to us."

Before the big move, they'd found a responsible new owner for his basset hound. Cody could still see the question in George's sad brown eyes when his enthusiastic new owner drove him away.

"Cody!" Emily tugged at his vest and tried to pull him away from the counter. "Can I whack a mole? Can I? Can I?"

Cody had no idea why she always had to ask every question three times. She must have inherited that habit from the alien side of her family. What a pain!

"Okay," he said. "But first we have to buy some tokens."

He deposited the five-dollar bill in the changer, then gave her a handful of tokens. "Half for you, half for me." He smiled as sweetly as he knew how. Emily glared.

"I can divide, you know. And five is definitely not half of 20."

What was up with kids these days? Cody shook his head. He hadn't learned division until the end of second grade. He gave Emily five more tokens and watched her wrestle her way through the crowd to her favorite game. There was nothing the little alien child loved more than bopping moles with a padded mallet.

Cody jingled the remaining ten tokens in his pocket. He needed 564 tickets to trade for the basset hound. He glanced back at the velvet hounds in the case. There were gray ones and red ones and brown ones, like George. The plush brown hound squatted on its haunches with its big ears drooping down to its front paws, just like George used to do. He had to have it.

Cody settled in front of a target game. He slipped a token into the slot and took aim at one of the targets. He pulled the trigger. Ping! One down. He took aim again. Ping! Another one down. After about five minutes, 20 tickets clicked out of the machine. Only 544 more to go!

A little while later, Emily appeared at his side, tugging on his vest.

Cody was getting exasperated. "Can't you see I'm busy here?"

She pursed her lips and twirled her pinky around a blond curl. Cody hated it when she did that. It meant "I need help."

"Come on." He grabbed her hand and half pulled her across the room. "Look," he said, as he stuck two of his tokens in the Whac-A-Mole® machine. "It's easy. All you have to do is pick up the mallet and bop them on their chubby little heads."

Cody held the mallet up, ready to whack the first mole that dared to show its face. He spent the next five minutes pounding mole holes, just after the moles disappeared every time.

"Man!" he said. "This is intense. No wonder you needed help."

Emily shook her head and held up a fat roll of tickets. "I didn't need help with that. I need help finding the restroom. I gotta go."

Cody hissed. He'd wasted two tokens on the stupid moles, and the pesky little alien with the ultrafast reflexes already had a wad of tickets twice as big as his.

Once he'd deposited Emily back in front of the faster-than-light moles, he headed for the Skee-Ball® alleys. He used up his last tokens rolling wooden balls into holes. Cody took his string of tickets to the counter. A girl with long black hair took his tickets and carelessly tossed them atop a scale. The scale registered 525. He didn't have enough!

"What do ya want?" The girl asked while popping her gum.

Cody stared blindly at the other items in the glass case. The only thing he really wanted was George. The stuffed basset hound wasn't George, but it would remind him of his buddy. Then Cody remembered. Emily!

"Hold on!" he told the girl. "I'll be right back."

"Em!" He spotted her heading for the Candy Crane® game. "I need a few more tickets. Can I have some of yours?"

Emily shook her head and stared down at the carpet. "I already spent them all."

Cody felt like she'd punched him. He should have known. The little alien girl would probably be curling her blond hair in front of the fake-fur mirror tonight. As he turned away, he felt a tug on his vest.

"I spent them on this." Emily held up a brown velvet basset hound. Its sad eyes looked up at Cody. "I thought you might be missing George."

"Em!" Cody exclaimed. "I can't believe you did that for me. You aren't such a bad little alien—I mean sister—after all!"

 ## Comprehension Check

**1.** What does Cody think would be better than an afternoon at the arcade?

**2.** Why does Cody want to trade his tickets for a stuffed basset hound?

**3.** How do you think Emily feels about her big brother, Cody? Why?

**4.** Do you think the stuffed basset hound will help Cody get over having to give away George? Why or why not?

# Doomed in Detention

*by Rusty Fischer*

Jill Perry hated staying after school for detention. Especially when she hadn't done anything wrong in the first place! Was it her fault her bike got a flat tire on the way to school and made her late? Now she was stuck in detention for a full hour!

Unfortunately, the detention teacher that day was Mrs. Nelson, the most strict teacher in school. That's exactly why Mrs. Nelson was stuck watching over the kids in detention so often. She was perfect for it!

Jill listened as Mrs. Nelson read the detention rules out loud. She emphasized the last rule over and over: no talking at any time!

"If you talk in this detention center," she said, peering over the tops of her reading glasses, "if you make so much as a peep, you will spend tomorrow afternoon in here as well—and for twice as long. That's two hours! So I suggest you think twice before whispering to your neighbor."

Jill didn't want to whisper anything to her neighbor, Sammy Jones. If Mrs. Nelson was the worst detention center teacher, Sammy was definitely the worst neighbor. He was a troublemaker with a capital *T*.

Jill looked at Sammy. Sammy looked right back, sending a shiver down her spine as she opened her math book and started her homework. While she began graphing coordinates, she heard Sammy fiddling with the pockets and zippers of his grungy backpack, zipping up one, unzipping another. Each time she would turn to give him a dirty look, he would give her an even dirtier stare right back!

Jill waited for Mrs. Nelson to scold Sammy, but she was all the way at the front of the room, bending over a big cookbook with her reading glasses perched at the tip of her nose. She completely ignored Sammy's zipping and unzipping.

Eventually Sammy found what he was looking for and the zipping ended. It was replaced by a new sound that irritated Jill even more: the chattering and squeaking of a real, live mouse!

Jill watched in disbelief as Sammy petted the mouse as if it were his very best friend. He kept holding the mouse out toward her, getting it a little closer each time. She looked to the front of the class for help from Mrs. Nelson. All she saw was the top of Mrs. Nelson's frizzy gray hair above the big cookbook she held in front of her face.

Jill wanted to scream. To shout. To yell! She wanted to cry out for someone to help her get rid of Sammy and his mouse, but she was afraid to make any noise. She could not stand another afternoon in the detention center.

Finally, Sammy reached into his backpack and brought out a chunk of cheeseburger. Sweat broke out on Jill's forehead as she watched Sammy wave the piece of meat under the mouse's twitching nose. Then he tossed it onto her desk! It splattered with a sound no mouse could ignore. She tried flicking it off, but a splotch of leftover ketchup held the burger there like a blob of glue. She heard the excited mouse squeak. She watched in horror as Sammy tossed the fat mouse right onto her cheeseburger-decorated desk.

Despite the rules that had been drilled into her by Mrs. Nelson, Jill screamed at the top of her lungs—for a full minute! It was the loudest sound she had ever made in her life.

Fortunately, the mouse seemed to hate noise as much as Mrs. Nelson. It bolted away from Jill, straight toward the front of the room. Mrs. Nelson clutched her cookbook to her chest. She stood up to see who had dared to break the silence of detention center. What she didn't see was Sammy's king-sized mouse charging toward her desk. As if it had spied all of that luscious food on the cover of Mrs. Nelson's cookbook, the mouse scrambled up the leg of her desk and scampered toward her. Now it was the teacher's turn to break the rules. She screamed!

Jill breathed a sigh of relief. Sammy and his mouse were on their way to visit the principal. And Mrs. Nelson couldn't give her more detention. If she did, the strict teacher would have to give herself two hours of detention, too!

 # Comprehension Check

**1.** Why is Jill in detention?

**2.** What will happen if Mrs. Nelson catches a student talking during detention?

**3.** Sammy pulls a mouse out of his backpack. What other things do you think a boy like Sammy might have in his pack?

**4.** Why do you think the mouse runs toward Mrs. Nelson?

# Nestor's Science Lesson

*by Kim T. Griswell*

"Mr. Bee! Mr. Bee!" Nestor Needleman waved his hand in the air. His teacher, Mr. Bezelbaum, lifted his bushy left eyebrow ever so slightly. Then he pointed at Henrietta Jacobsen, who pushed her glasses up on her nose and sat up straighter.

"Limestone," she smirked at Nestor, "is a sedimentary rock composed of calcium carbonate, calcite, and carbonate mud. Most limestones contain fossils."

"Mr. Bee!" Nestor waved his hand again.

"Yes, Nestor?" His voice had that why-did-I-get-out-of-bed-this-morning whine in it.

"That's not exactly correct."

"Oh, really?" He waved his hand toward the other students. "Then why don't you enlighten us."

"Limestone is really a citrus-tasting rock, kind of like lemonstone, but greener. It's found primarily in Ireland—usually next to patches of shamrocks."

The classroom erupted.

Henrietta took off her glasses, puffed a breath on them, and then cleaned them on the tail of her T-shirt.

Mr. Bezelbaum ignored Nestor and took another rock from the box on his desk.

"How about this one? Wolframite."

"Ooh, ooh!" Nestor's hand shot up again.

Mr. Bezelbaum tried to ignore him, but no other hands went up. He scrunched up his mouth until it disappeared beneath his mustache, then nodded.

"Well, there were these Russians out with their wolfhounds looking for rocks, and they—"

"Um, there *are* major deposits of wolframite in Russia, Mr. Bezelbaum, but I really don't think there are any wolfhounds involved," Henrietta interjected.

"Yes. Thank you, Henrietta."

Mr. Bezelbaum stroked his mustache and stared into the box. "Do I dare?" he asked. Then he looked at the ceiling as if waiting for an answer to fall from the fluorescent lights. When none came, he sighed and picked up another rock.

"Serpentine."

His eyes dared Nestor to raise his hand. Nestor, of course, took the dare.

"Well, it's called serpentine because the first guy who saw it thought it was a green snake coiled on top of a rock, but it wasn't. It was just a rock."

"Just…a rock." Mr. Bezelbaum tossed the serpentine back in the box.

"When you polish serpentine, it looks like marble, not a green snake," Henrietta said. "One type is mined in Canada, Russia, and South Africa."

"Thank you, Henrietta. Why don't you choose the next specimen?"

Henrietta stood and went up to the desk.

"Sillimanite," she said primly, holding up a pale green glassy rock.

"Well?" Mr. Bezelbaum waited. "Anyone have a serious comment to make about the mineral sillimanite?" His mustache twitched as he watched Nestor from the corner of his eye.

When no hands shot up, Nestor stood slowly.

Mr. Bezelbaum's left eyebrow started twitching in time with his mustache.

"I believe that sillimanite is an uncommon mineral. It is found in central Europe, Brazil, and the United States."

Mr. Bezelbaum almost fell off his desk. "Why, Nestor. That's absolutely correct."

"Uh, excuse me." Henrietta raised her hand. "Mr. Bezelbaum?"

He nodded and smiled. "Yes, Henrietta? You have something to add?"

"Well, I hate to contradict my learned classmate, but I believe that SILL-ee-man-ite," she slowly mispronounced the word, "is actually found primarily in fifth-grade classrooms—in close proximity to Nestor Needleman."

"Henrietta!" Nestor beamed. "You finally got one right!"

 ## Comprehension Check

**1.** What connections does Nestor make to come up with his wacky descriptions of the rocks?

**2.** What is Mr. Bezelbaum trying to teach his class?

**3.** How does Mr. Bezelbaum feel about Nestor's comments? What clues does the story give about his feelings?

**4.** Does Henrietta's final rock description surprise you? Why or why not?

# Slimed at the Cinema

*by Rusty Fischer*

Darnel and Trevor Cummings couldn't believe it when their mom actually let them see a midnight movie! Especially one about a giant jar of angry strawberry jam that couldn't stop growing and ended up covering an entire city in sticky, red goop! They also couldn't believe that they were the only two people in the whole movie theater when the house lights finally went down. They thought the place would be packed. After all, who wouldn't want to see a two-hour movie about killer strawberry jam?

It wasn't long before they realized why they were the only two people in the theater. The movie was awful!

"Darnel!" Trevor groaned as loudly as he pleased. No one was around to shush him. "This is the worst movie I've ever seen. How come you dragged me here?"

"Me?" Darnel moaned even louder. "You're the one who picked it!"

The two brothers looked at each other and grinned. Since they were identical twins, they often felt that they were looking in a mirror every time they saw each other face-to-face. They had the same green eyes; the same smooth, dark skin; and even the same goofy grin. Besides being brothers, Darnel and Trevor were best friends.

After complaining about how bad the movie was for a little while longer, the two tired twins settled in to watch it anyway. There was no way they were calling their mom to come get them early the one time she finally caved in and let them see a midnight movie! No matter how bad the movie was, they planned to enjoy it.

It wasn't long, however, before the two brothers, full of popcorn and candy and up way past their bedtime, fell fast asleep. With their feet propped up on the empty seats in front of them, they dozed peacefully.

Trevor woke up first. He had noticed a sickly sweet smell that made his nostrils twitch. He didn't know exactly what the smell was, but for some reason, it made him want a piece of toast. He blinked his eyes and looked at the flickering movie screen. A quaking, shaking blob of evil strawberry jam rolled right over a fake-looking model of some city, destroying it completely.

Then, to Trevor's amazement, the blob kept coming. It oozed closer and closer to the screen until it rolled right off the screen and onto the theater floor! Trevor shook Darnel awake as the strawberry blob oozed its way up the aisle. It slimed under, into, and right over the seats in front of them.

"We've got to get out of here!" Trevor shouted, pulling at Darnel's sleeve.

The brothers scrambled over their seats and hit the ground running, trying to keep ahead of the advancing blob. It was fast, much faster than a huge glob of jam should have been. It sucked at the heels of their sneakers as they burst out of the double doors and into the lobby. The blob oozed right behind them.

Darnel and Trevor sprinted over the velvet theater ropes. Movie posters stared out at them from greasy plastic frames. Video games beeped and clicked as if it were just a normal night. Through the glass doors, they could see a few cars in the parking lot. Nothing would block their way once they were outside with the doors shut behind them. They slammed into the double doors, but the doors didn't budge.

"They're locked!" Trevor gasped. "What are we gonna do?"

"I don't know. You think of something!" Darnel yelled.

They banged and rattled and kicked at the doors, but nothing happened. Turning around, they saw the blob moving closer and closer. Just as it touched the toes of their sneakers, both boys shut their eyes in terror.

"Darnel! Trevor!"

When they dared to open their eyes, they saw their mother standing over them.

Darnel looked at Trevor. Trevor looked at Darnel. Where was the blob?

"That's the last time I let you two see a midnight movie. All you did was eat junk food and fall asleep. You could have done that at home!"

Darnel and Trevor looked at each other again. They checked for bits of strawberry goop on their shoes. When they didn't find any, they smiled. It looked like one bad movie had led to one really bad nightmare!

##  Comprehension Check

**1.** Why are the brothers the only ones in the movie theater?

**2.** Why are Trevor and Darnel so sleepy during the movie?

**3.** Do you think Trevor and Darnel could have both been having the same nightmare? Why or why not?

**4.** Do you think the boys' mom will let them go to another midnight movie? Why or why not?

# Weird Hannah

*by Kim T. Griswell*

The weird thing about Hannah Hunter was that, well, she was weird. Different. Odd. Unusual with a capital *U*. She'd moved to Jonesboro at the end of the school year, so no one really had time to get to know her before summer sunshine sent them all outdoors to join baseball teams, kick soccer balls, and swim.

On the first day of the new school year, she showed up in a pair of bell-bottom blue jeans and a tie-dyed T-shirt. Dozens of bracelets jangled on her thin wrists. She looked like something out of the 1970s. Nobody really knew what to say to her.

Hannah, on the other hand, seemed articulate, as if she always knew exactly what to say.

When Laura Juster informed Sheika Wright that her new dress was way too juvenile for fifth grade, Hannah walked up to Sheika and said, "Knock, knock."

Laura rolled her eyes, but Sheika said, "Who's there?" She'd have said anything to change the subject.

"Orange." Hannah grinned.

"I know you're new here," Laura interrupted, "but we stopped telling knock-knock jokes two years ago."

The girls nearby nodded, but Hannah's brown eyes just kept sparkling.

"Orange who?" Sheika asked. Better to keep Laura focused on Hannah now that she'd pointed her sharp tongue at someone else.

"Orange you glad you didn't put your shirt on backward this morning like Laura did?"

She said it so loudly that everyone in class stopped talking and turned to stare. Laura's face turned the color of a ripe cherry. She fled to the girl's room without even asking for a hall pass. The class erupted.

"That's enough, class," their teacher instructed. "Please take your seats."

Hannah slid into a seat right at the front of the room, and Sheika took the one behind her.

"Thanks," she whispered.

The next day, Hannah wore ruby red shoes with three-inch platforms. On her right cheek she had a washable rose tattoo with red glitter on top of it.

"Look at the way she dresses! Don't you think that's weird?" Laura asked.

Sheika shook her head. "She's different in a nutty kind of way, but what's wrong with having your own style?"

Mickey Lawrence, who could never resist teasing a "newbie," called across the room, "Hey, Dorothy! Hasn't anyone told you you're not in Kansas anymore?"

Hannah gave Mickey a friendly smile. "Knock, knock," she said nicely.

"Who's there?" Mickey asked with a worried look.

"Wooden shoe," Hannah replied.

"Wooden shoe who?"

"Wooden shoe like to trade that straw coming out of your head for a brain?"

Mickey stuffed his scruffy blond hair back under his baseball cap and opened a book. He stuck his nose in its pages and didn't look up again until lunchtime.

Sheika practically ran to catch up with Hannah, who was already in the lunchroom. "Mind if I sit with you?" she asked.

"That would be superexcellent." Hannah flashed a smile.

"You really have a way with words," Sheika said as she set her plastic tray on the table and sat down. "You always seem to know just what to say when someone's being obnoxious. My mind freezes up, and nothing will come out of my mouth when someone's being mean."

Hannah shrugged. "My mom always says that humor takes the sting out of the biggest hornet."

"So you use knock-knock jokes to stop someone from teasing you?" Bob Bruchac asked as he pulled out a chair and sat down across from them.

Hannah dipped a carrot stick into a mound of ketchup. "Pretty much," she said. "But there's a bit more to it."

"Like what?" Sheika edged closer.

"Like you have to realize that teasers try to get attention by making someone else look bad. To take the sting out of their put-downs, you have to turn the tables."

"Hornets like to sting, but they don't enjoy being stung back." Sheika nodded.

"So how do you come up with those jokes of yours?" asked Bob.

Hannah munched a few bites of carrot stick. "Observation."

"Observation?" the others asked at the same time.

Hannah nodded. "I look carefully at the person bugging me until I find something funny. I use what I find to turn the joke back on them. Works every time."

Sheika and Bob weren't the only ones who were tired of being picked on by kids like Laura and Mickey. After a few more knock-knock jokes, Hannah had a whole table of classmates joining her for lunch.

"Look. It's the losers' table," Laura said spitefully as she walked past.

"Knock, knock," Hannah said.

"Forget it." Laura's cheeks reddened. "You're not going to knock me down with another one of those dumb kiddie jokes," she said.

"Who's there?" the kids at Hannah's table asked together.

Everyone in the cafeteria turned.

"Ida Rather."

"Ida Rather who?" the table chorused.

Laura looked as if she wanted to dump the mashed potatoes and mystery meat on her tray over Hannah's head. She stalked away before Hannah could finish.

Bob nudged her. "So what were you going to say?"

Hannah's dark eyes twinkled. "Ida rather be sitting here surrounded by 'losers,'" she said, making quotation marks with her fingers, "than standing there all by myself."

 # Comprehension Check

**1.** What makes Hannah seem weird to the other students?

**2.** Hannah is described as "articulate." Based on clues from the story, what do you think that means?

**3.** How does Hannah turn the tables on the teasers?

**4.** Whom would you rather have for a friend: Hannah or Laura? Why?

# Helmet Head

*by Kim T. Griswell*

"Mom," Gina called as she pulled on her wrist guards and knee and elbow pads, then clomped to the door in her in-line skates, "I'm heading down to the beach!"

"Don't forget your helmet!" her mother answered.

"Mom!" Gina groaned. "You know I'm careful. I'll be absolutely safe without my helmet."

"No helmet, no beach." Her mother wandered into the living room wiping red ink off her palm.

Gina's mother was an editor; she prepared books for publication, checking every punctuation mark, every snippet of grammar, every seemingly insignificant detail. Since she'd been trained to notice details, she always did, especially when it came to safety.

"Better to be safe than sorry," she said.

"You're talking in clichés again, Mom," Gina teased.

"Oops. How about a simile instead?" She stopped rubbing at the ink and got a glassy look in her eyes; then she said, "A head without a helmet is like a raw egg waiting to be cracked."

"Gross!" Gina reached for the sleek black and purple helmet hanging by its chin strap from the coat hook. She detested the way it squashed her hair; she'd have helmet head when she got to the beach. Not a pretty sight!

Once outside, Gina skated toward the main road, then turned south. Wind smacked her in the face, flinging back the spongy red curls that spilled from beneath her helmet. Pine needles rained down, jabbing into the ground all around her. That's some wind, she thought.

She saw Joel Crowder skating toward her. He hunkered down, his blades sweeping side to side as he skimmed along the walk.

"Hey! Joel! Where you going? The beach is the other way." Gina waved.

Joel shook his head. "I've been eating sand for half an hour. I'm going home."

Gina shrugged. Wimp.

When she reached the concrete promenade along the beach, Gina turned south again. This time, the wind nearly blew her off her feet. She grabbed for the rail that ran along the paved walkway. Once her blades stopped wobbling, she leaned forward and rested her hands on her knees to catch her breath. Then she stood, shielding her eyes as she looked down the beach.

Along the promenade, blowing sand turned the air thick; it scoured the concrete benches and light poles. The wind made the chimneys moan like bagpipes.

Gina tasted sand. The grit on the promenade made the footing treacherous; she'd have to be more attentive than usual. To compensate for the wind pushing against her, she shoved off the rail and skated with her head down. She kept her eyes open just a crack to keep sand from blowing into them, but there was no avoiding it. The sand blew so thick and heavy that she kept her mouth shut in a thin line, feeling as if she might suffocate. Joel's not such a wimp after all, she admitted as bits of sand scratched her eyes.

A bicyclist lumbered past, heading in the opposite direction. The loose vinyl poncho he wore kept flying into his face, as if pulled up by an invisible hand. She watched as he attempted to fight it off.

"Look out!" a deep voice yelled.

Gina turned just in time to see a shingle flying toward her. Her heart skip-hopped as she ducked. The shingle bounced off her helmet, making it ring like plastic wind chimes. She watched wide-eyed as the shingle splintered into three pieces on the sidewalk. The smell of cedar filled the air. A few houses down, two carpenters teetered on a scaffolding that shook with each gust of wind. One of the men climbed down and sprinted toward her.

"Are you okay?" he asked. He put a hand on her shoulder and peered into her eyes.

She nodded, though her head still rang and her knees felt as choppy as wind-tossed waves.

"I've lived here 30 years and I've never been caught out in anything like this," he said. "Weatherman claims it's the tail end of a hurricane that hit Mexico a few days ago."

"If this is the tail, I'd hate to see what the head looked like." Gina fought to keep the tremor from her voice as she looked at the splintered shingle on the sidewalk.

The carpenter followed her gaze. "It's a good thing you were wearing that helmet." He picked up a piece of the shattered shingle.

"You're right. Without this thing," she tapped her helmet, "my head might've looked like a cracked egg!"

The man's skin went pale beneath his summer tan. "That would not be a pretty sight," he said.

Gina tightened her chin strap. Helmet head isn't so bad after all, she decided as she skated toward home.

 ## Comprehension Check

1. Why does Gina's mother pay such close attention to details?

2. Why doesn't Gina want to wear her helmet?

3. When Gina sees Joel, she thinks he's a wimp for going home. Why does she change her mind?

4. What other sport can you think of that uses special gear like the helmets skaters wear? Why do you think this gear is required?

# Grandfather's Wisdom

*by Kim T. Griswell*

While Rob and Erin focused their eyes on the turquoise sky and the craggy mountains towering over them, Jimmy Yellow Owl watched the trail.

"Hurry up!" Rob motioned from the trail ahead.

Jimmy shook his head. "If you keep rushing ahead like that, you're going to hurry us right into a grizzly."

"Grizzly!" Erin's curly brown hair nearly whipped Jimmy in the face as she turned. "You didn't say anything about grizzlies."

Rob and Erin had recently moved to West Glacier from Philadelphia. Though he was a city kid, Rob seemed to think he knew a lot about the mountains. Jimmy quickly realized that he didn't know anything about the wild trails of Montana.

Jimmy nodded. "Sure. There are grizzlies in these woods."

Rob's eyes narrowed. "You ever seen one?"

"No." Jimmy shook his head. "Grandfather Yellow Owl taught me how to make sure I never do."

"Well," Rob tightened the waist strap on his pack, "if you haven't seen one, then as far as I'm concerned, they're nothing but some old man's imaginings."

Ignoring Rob's insult, Jimmy kept watching for signs of a bear. When none appeared, he relaxed enough to enjoy the sun warming the fog from his breath. As he walked, he chatted with Erin, as much to make noise and alert any bears to their presence as to learn more about her life in the city.

"You guys pipe down!" Rob called back. "How are we going to see any wildlife if you keep chattering like a couple of squirrels?"

"Grandfather says that noise can be your best protection in the woods," Jimmy said.

Rob snorted. "I'm beginning to wonder if you have a thought in your head your grandfather didn't put there!"

A coldness settled in Jimmy's gut. Some city kids have no respect!

As they continued up the trail, only the distant rumble of Twin Falls broke the silence. Jimmy scanned the trail again; his eyes had lost focus as angry thoughts buzzed through his head. Suddenly, his gaze sharpened as his boot nearly tramped into a dark pile studded with pieces of red berries.

Bear scat! He held out a hand to stop Erin.

"What?" she whispered.

Jimmy stepped back and let his gaze wander along the trail. Looking back, he noticed a tuft of gray, grizzled fur caught in the bark of a tree. Nearby, he noted a fallen log with its side gashed open. Beetles scurried in and out of the raw, exposed wood.

"Go back down the trail," he said. "Quietly."

She opened her mouth, then shut it and nodded as her eyes went from his face to the bear droppings.

Jimmy turned; his chest tightened as if clutched by powerful claws. Rob had just topped the rise, but instead of hurrying on as he'd done all morning, his feet seemed to have turned to mud, sticking him fast at the crest.

"Bear?" Jimmy asked just loudly enough for Rob to hear. Rob nodded. "Has it seen you?" Rob shook his head no.

Taking a deep breath, Jimmy inched toward the rise. As he reached Rob's side, he took in the scene quickly. Two tawny cubs peered from the trees about 50 feet away. Just down the slope, the mother grizzly clawed at a decaying log, searching for grubs.

"Back away really slowly," Jimmy said. "Don't make a sound."

Rob shook his head. "I'm not backing away slowly," he said softly. "I'm running!"

"Look at her." Jimmy nodded at the mother grizzly's massive shoulders. "She can run as fast as a racehorse. Can you?"

Rob's face paled. He shook his head no, then began to back down the rise. Jimmy matched him silent footstep for silent footstep, listening for any new sound from the grizzly now hidden from sight. The slightest huff or snort might mean she had sensed their presence and was about to head their way. At the bottom of the rise, he nudged Rob's arm and jerked his head.

"Let's get out of here," he whispered.

They ran until they caught up with Erin. Jimmy's lungs burned. Rob's face was as red as a ripe apple.

When Rob could breathe again, he turned to Jimmy. "I guess you saved my life," he said. "How did you know what to do?"

Jimmy huffed as angrily as a bear. "If you'd listened to a word I said earlier, you'd know."

"Your grandfather?" The fear in Rob's eyes melted into admiration. "I guess he knows a lot more about the woods than I do."

Jimmy grinned. "You finally said something I can agree with!"

 ## Comprehension Check

1. Why does Jimmy keep such a close watch on the trail as he hikes?

2. How does Jimmy think Rob feels about his elders?

3. From the information in the story, what culture do you think Jimmy comes from? Why?

4. This story shares some information about dealing with grizzly encounters in the woods. If you were going for a hike in grizzly country, what should you do to prepare?

# Natural Habitats

*by Kim T. Griswell*

Victor Yazzi kicked at the spiny tumbleweed with a dust-covered boot. Like everything else in the Arizona scrub, it looked dead, sucked dry. Overhead, the sun burned like a blowtorch in the turquoise sky. Sweat stopped at the red patterned scarf tied around his forehead, keeping his eyes clear.

"Wait up!" His new friend called. Monroe Jones tottered along the rock-strewn path behind Victor. The heat made the coffee brown skin of his face take on the same shade of red as his football jersey.

Just before school had let out for summer, Monroe had moved to the Arizona desert from Los Angeles. Victor had decided to take him hiking on the Navajo reservation just outside their small town. So far, it looked as if his city friend needed a few tips on surviving in the desert. Victor uncapped his canteen and handed it to Monroe.

"This isn't the city," Victor said. "You shouldn't come out here without water."

Monroe gurgled in agreement and slugged down so much water that Victor grabbed the canteen away from him.

"If you guzzle it all now, we'll be as dry as this thing by the time we get home," he said as he nudged the tumbleweed with the toe of his boot.

"Sorry," Monroe said. He wiped his mouth on his shirttail, adding another wet spot to the perspiration stains already there. "This is great!" he said, sweeping his arm out to include the rose- and ocher-streaked mesas casting shadows over them. "No traffic. No crime. Nobody trying to pick a fight. Just a bossy trail guide."

Victor shook his head. "You wouldn't survive in *my* habitat for an hour without me for a guide."

Monroe shrugged. "Yeah, well, I'd like to see you survive in *my* habitat."

Victor tucked his long, straight, black hair behind his ears and started walking. "Tell you what," he said. "If I ever go to L.A., you can be *my* guide." He looped his canteen strap over one shoulder. "Until then, I'm in charge."

They hiked silently for a while, trying to ignore the sun scouring the thoughts from their heads. Finally, Victor halted in the shadow of a boulder.

"Rest stop!" Monroe said, scooting around a rock in search of shade.

"Watch out for rattlers!" Victor warned. "They like to hide in these cool shadows just like we do."

Only seconds later, Monroe yelped. "Snake!"

"Just stand still till I get there," Victor said, stepping cautiously around the boulder. No warning rattle shook the silence. All he could hear was Monroe's startled breathing and the cry of a hawk circling overhead. "Where is it?" Victor asked, moving closer. He eyed Monroe's canvas high-tops and was glad for the thick leather of his boots. Canvas would be no protection at all from a snakebite.

"There!" Monroe pointed, shuddering. "I think it's a cobra."

Victor snorted. "There are no cobras in Arizona."

"It hissed at me!" Monroe insisted.

At last Victor sighted the snake. It was brown, with darker brown blotches down its back. Its heavy snout came to a point, and it had a heavy keel along the top. It curled about three feet away from Monroe's left sneaker. As they watched, the snake spread its jaws and neck and hissed again. Instead of drawing back, Victor vaulted toward it, landing in front of Monroe.

"Are you crazy?" Monroe superglued himself to Victor's shadow as a cloud of dust rose around Victor's boots.

The snake began to writhe, flinging back its head as if in agony. Then it flopped onto its back and lay still; its tongue lolled out of its mouth.

Monroe peered over Victor's shoulder. "If I hadn't seen it with my own eyes, I wouldn't believe it! You scared that thing to death." He patted Victor's shoulder. "Thanks. I thought I was a goner."

Victor couldn't help laughing.

"What's so funny?"

Victor nudged the snake with the toe of his boot. "It's not dead," he said. "It's playing dead."

"Huh? Since when do cobras play dead?"

Victor squatted beside the snake. "They don't. But hognose snakes do. What a ham!" He picked the snake up. Its body hung limp and lifeless from his hand.

"Looks dead to me." Monroe said as he inched closer.

"Watch this." Victor put the snake back down and rolled it onto its belly. Immediately, it rolled back over.

"Look out!" Monroe jumped back again.

"It's perfectly harmless—as long as you can stand bad acting," Victor said with a grin. "Guess you do need a guide."

This time, the red in Monroe's face didn't come from the heat. "Looks like we both know how to survive in our natural habitats."

Victor pointed at the hognose. "And so does he!" he said.

 ## Comprehension Check

1. What things does Monroe do in this story that endanger him?

2. Why does Monroe think Victor would need a guide in Los Angeles?

3. Victor says that the snake is not a cobra. Why do you think he would know this?

4. Based on clues in the story, how do you think Monroe's and Victor's lives differ?

# Downhill Dare

*by Rusty Fischer*

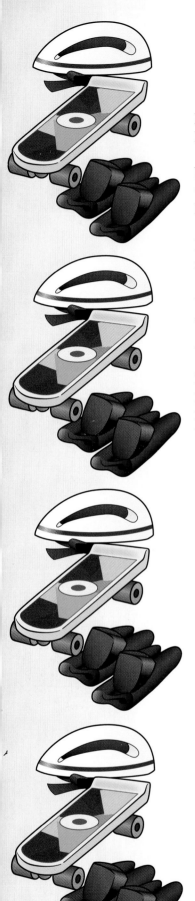

Cyrus Billings couldn't believe it when his dad gave him a new skateboard for his birthday. He had asked for one, sure, but when did that ever matter? Last year he'd asked for a moped and all he got was a pair of pajamas!

It wasn't just any old skateboard either. It was the top of the line, the best of the best, the kind of skateboard that made the other kids green with envy. Without even taking a bite of his birthday cake, Cyrus sprinted straight out the door, hopped on his board, and cruised all the way to Meyer's Hill.

All the skateboarders hung out at Meyer's Hill. It was a nasty, scary looking hill—the worst of the worst! It was the kind of hill that made all the kids green—with fear!

A couple of kids skated near the bottom of the hill, but no one ever went to the top. He coasted to where they were, careful to go very slowly, just so everyone could admire his brand-new board.

Most of the kids oohed and aahed, but someone behind him started laughing. Who in the world could laugh at such a fantastic new skateboard? Cyrus turned around and found out. Murphy Newman was laughing, that's who! Murphy Newman was the meanest, toughest shark of a skateboarder to ever come around Meyer's Hill. Cyrus didn't need anybody, least of all Murphy Newman, laughing at his new skateboard.

"What are you laughing at?" he asked, wheeling smoothly over to Murphy.

"You and that dorky skateboard," Murphy said.

"If anyone's skateboard needs to get laughed at, it's yours," Cyrus said. He looked down at Murphy's old, beat-up board.

"Mine may not be brand-new from the toy store like yours," Murphy sneered, "but at least the guy riding it knows how to skate!"

Cyrus and Murphy stood without blinking, their boards nose to nose; then a meaner than usual look passed over Murphy's face.

"I'll bet my skateboard against your skateboard that I can get to the bottom of Meyer's Hill faster than you can!" he dared.

Cyrus looked up at the top of the hill and gulped. It was as close to vertical as a hill could be, so steep some vehicles spit and spluttered trying to pull up it. He had only had his skateboard for a few minutes. Now he had to race it down the scariest hill since Mount Everest? He knew he should refuse to race, but the other kids egged him on.

"Come on, Cy! Show him what your board can do!" they chanted.

Cyrus reluctantly followed Murphy up the hill. At the very top, he held onto his skateboard like it was his only friend. He stood next to Murphy, looking down at the rest of the skaters standing at the bottom. They looked as small as ants.

Cyrus looked over at Murphy. A line of sweat beaded above his lip; he didn't look as confident as he had at the bottom of the hill.

Both boys put their boards down reluctantly. Each one planted one foot in the center of his board. They leaned forward, looking down the hill that dropped away like a ski slope. Neither boy pushed off.

This is ridiculous, Cyrus thought. We'll crash and end up with a major case of road rash. He looked down at Murphy's board. "You know," he said, "I was just joking about your board. It's pretty cool, even if it is old."

"Yeah, well," Murphy muttered, "it's too late now. You already took the dare. Besides, everyone's watching. We've got to go, right?"

Cyrus looked down the hill and nodded his head in agreement. "I guess so."

As Cyrus racked his brain for a way out of their predicament, a chant rose from below: "Chicken! Chicken!"

Now they were cooked. There was no way out of this, not without being labeled "chicken" for life. Swallowing hard, Cyrus got ready to ride Meyer's Hill. Then he had a flash.

"You know, Murphy, those guys have got a lot of nerve calling you a chicken."

"Yeah. I can't let them do that, can I?"

Cyrus shrugged.

"Who are you calling chicken?" Murphy shouted, pointing a finger at the kids down below. "When I get down there, we'll see who's a chicken and who's going to be my next challenger."

The chanting below died down instantly as the kids dispersed, flying off on their boards as fast as they could.

Murphy looked at Cyrus and grinned. "Looks like our audience is gone. Truce?"

Cyrus nodded.

"You know, I could teach you a thing or two about riding that new board of yours," Murphy said, kicking his board up into his hand.

"You could?"

Murphy nodded. "But we'll have to be on level ground first."

"Level ground sounds good to me!" Cyrus said, picking up his board. "Let's go!"

##  Comprehension Check

1. Why is Cyrus so surprised to get a new skateboard for his birthday?

2. Why doesn't Cyrus want to skate down Meyer's Hill?

3. Do you think that Murphy really wants to skate down Meyer's Hill? Why or why not?

4. What kind of person does Cyrus think Murphy is at the beginning of the story? Do you think his opinion changes after what happens on the hill? Why or why not?

# Storm Chasers!

*by Kim T. Griswell*

When Mary asked Jimmi to help her track a storm that was building in the next county, he thought it sounded a bit crazy. When his family moved from California to Oklahoma, he'd been glad to trade the rumble and shake of earthquakes for the occasional crack of a lightning storm. Then his mom had made him study the rules for tornado safety. He'd learned enough to know that chasing after one wasn't part of any emergency preparedness plan.

"Aren't we supposed to get in a basement or something?" asked Jimmi.

Mary shook her head. "The weather service issued a watch, not a warning. Besides, many experts chase storms. Did you know that Ben Franklin was a storm chaser?"

"Ben Franklin? The guy with the kite and the key?"

Mary nodded. "One time he chased a whirlwind on his horse for almost a mile!"

"Okay, so one of the founding fathers was nuts. Does that mean we have to be?"

Mary shifted the video camera to her other shoulder. "He wasn't nuts. He was a scientist. You might even say he was a meteorologist, since he studied the weather. And if I want to be one as soon as I finish college, then I can't be afraid of a bit of research. Besides, storm chasers know how to be careful around twisters. But we might get a few bumps and bruises from hailstones. You're not chicken, are you?"

Jimmi watched the horizon. It was turning green. The late spring air felt as thick as a San Francisco fog, but hot instead of cold. Oklahoma was in the middle of Tornado Alley, an area that stretched south to Texas and north to the Dakotas. Twisting, twirling storms zipped across the plains every spring and summer. From the look of the sky, Jimmi wondered if the weather service needed to update its watch to a warning.

The dry grass crackled as Mary walked across the field. She filmed and mumbled into the camera's microphone as she walked.

"The air is still. Kind of creepy," she said. "Cloud color is greenish. Conditions look right for a funnel to develop."

A whine began to come from the direction of town, like someone had just pulled the tail of a very big cat. Jimmi whirled around.

"The siren. Wow!" Mary's voice filled with excitement. "Now we'll get some pictures."

As if in response, the monstrous cloud began to dip down. First, it looked like a giant triangle hanging in the sky; then it reached for the ground.

Something that sounded like a train joined the blare of the siren. Jimmi could hardly hear Mary, though she stood right beside him. The sky began to spit pea-sized hailstones.

"Come on!" Jimmi shouted, holding his arms over his head to keep the cold stones from stinging his face. "Let's get out of here!"

"I've got to get this on film!" Mary pointed her camera toward the funnel. "We've got a funnel on the ground." She yelled into the microphone. "It's moving northeast, away from town, I think. Wait a minute. It's turning. Now it…it…"

Her voice trailed off and she lowered the camera. Her confidence crumpled like a popped balloon. "It doesn't look like it's moving anymore."

"That's good, isn't it?" asked Jimmi.

She shook her head. "No. It means the tornado is heading straight for us."

"What?" Jimmi felt like he'd been punched.

"We need to take cover." Mary took the camera from her shoulder and searched the area with her eyes.

"There's a big culvert that runs beneath the road just behind those trees." Jimmi pointed toward a line of tall cedars that were doing the twist.

Jimmi started running, with Mary at his heels. He glanced back over his shoulder. The funnel spread across the field like a giant vacuum cleaner hose, sucking up everything in its path. Dirt and debris filled the sky, so he couldn't really see exactly where the funnel touched the ground.

"Hurry!" He hooked his arm through Mary's and ran faster. The cedars tried to twist themselves out of the earth. Branches lashed Jimmi's face as he fought his way through.

"There it is!" Jimmi pointed toward a dry streambed that had turned into a river of icy pebbles. They slipped and slid through the treacherous hailstones. Jimmi heard a splintering crash behind them and turned just in time to see one of the cedars rip from the ground.

"Get in!" He shoved Mary toward the culvert and scrunched in after her. On hands and knees, they scrambled toward the middle of the giant metal pipe, ignoring the rocks that bit their hands and knees and the spiderwebs that clung to their faces. The roar filled the pipe and shook the ground so hard, Jimmi felt like he was back in California. Dirt and hail blasted from the streambed toward them. He turned away from the opening and tucked his head as low as it would go. Mary crouched behind him, hunched over her camera.

A few seconds later, the shaking stopped; the roar faded. It was over.

Mary looked up with a shaky smile. "Guess I've got a lot to learn about chasing storms," she said. "How'd you know this culvert was here?"

"My mom made me study up on tornado safety. Then I scouted the area to make sure I knew where all the safe places were." He shrugged. "Guess I'm a chicken, like you said."

"You know," Mary grinned, "chickens can be very useful birds!"

 ## Comprehension Check

1. Why does Mary want to chase the storm?

2. What part does Ben Franklin play in this story?

3. How does Jimmi know where to go when the tornado comes?

4. Jimmi moves from California, where there are earthquakes, to Oklahoma, where there are tornadoes. If you had to choose to live where there are either earthquakes or tornadoes, which would you choose? Why?

# Magic Enough for Me

*by Laura Purdie Salas*

On the airplane ride, my little brother Chip bounced up and down, kicked the seat in front of him, and looked out of the window. I sulked.

My friends believed I was lucky to go to southern Florida for Christmas. They said it would be like magic, that maybe I could go to the beach on Christmas Day. I watched the ground transform from white snow to ugly brown squares. Would I be able to find the magic of Christmas in those squares?

When I left Minnesota, the air was crisp with bare twigs dancing in the wind. When we got to Florida, the air was slow and moist, like a hot, wet blanket draped around my shoulders.

At Aunt Paula's house, Mom helped me unpack my rolling suitcase. I took out my brand-new sweater, the gray one with purple and pink reindeer embroidered across the front. I stretched my new pink pants out beside the sweater. I couldn't wait to wear my Christmas outfit.

The next day, Uncle Jim said, "A heat wave's coming just for you all."

My mom and dad sighed contentedly. I groaned. Mom gave me an admonishing look, and I pasted on a fake smile.

By Christmas Eve, perspiration had become my middle name. It was so steamy that I had to borrow a pair of ugly, bulky shorts from my cousin Edward. He was 13, two years older than me. I looked at my beautiful sweater. Would I be able to wear it for Christmas? Probably not, I decided as I pulled on Edward's baggy black and purple shorts.

Aunt Paula shooed us out to play.

"Enjoy this while it lasts," said my mom. She had her eyes closed and her head tilted to the sky like a sunflower, so she didn't see me glare at her.

"There's nothing to do here," I told Edward. "You can't go sledding or ice skating or have snowball fights or anything!"

"Stop whining," said Edward. "Anything you can do up there in Freezerland, we can do down here."

How do you explain the magic of Christmas to someone who lives in southern Florida? How do you describe snow angels, breath clouds, and lacy white trim on all the trees?

"Snow angels," I said. "I bet you can't make snow angels."

Maybe Edward felt sorry for me, or maybe Uncle Jim had lectured him. Either way, instead of making fun of me, he led me to the sandbox. Five minutes later, my shorts were full of sand and I itched all over.

"Nice try," I said, "but it's just not the same. Christmas in Minnesota is like magic. Christmas in Florida is hot, itchy, and boring."

I brushed myself off.

"Magic, huh? I'll show you some magic. Let's go sledding!" Edward proposed.

"Sledding? How?"

Edward dug out some skateboards. "Come on," he said, leading me to the top of a bike trail. As I closed my eyes and tried to imagine snow, sweat trickled down my back. I sank my fingers into the thick grass, pushed off, and bumped downhill.

For an instant, I felt cool as the breeze blew the sweat off my cheeks. Edward swerved into the grass at the bottom of the hill. When I tried to do the same, I slid off the skateboard and skidded along the ground. I tore Edward's ugly shorts in about seven different spots.

"Oh, well," I said, smiling away the pain, "thanks anyway."

Back at the house, I flopped onto the floor, centering myself over the air-conditioning vent. Cold air puffed on my stomach.

That night, we went to a midnight Christmas service. I wore a sundress borrowed from Aunt Paula that hung below my knees. Though the sun had gone down hours ago, it was still too muggy for my Christmas sweater. If there truly is a Santa Claus, I feel sorry for him, lugging around a huge sack of gifts and wearing that furry red suit in this heat.

In bed, I tossed and fidgeted.

In the morning, I woke up shivering, feeling as if I'd been miraculously transported home to Minnesota. The temperature must have plummeted overnight! I peered out the window, half expecting to see a layer of snow on the ground. No white snow gleamed outside the window. Even though it had turned as cold as the North Pole, I was still in Florida.

Aunt Paula stuck her head in the room. "Merry Christmas!" she said. "Dress warmly and come on down. It's time for breakfast and gifts."

I slipped into my pink pants and my reindeer sweater, feeling snug and warm.

When I got downstairs, a fire crackled in the fireplace, lights twinkled on the Christmas tree, presents piled beneath it. The smell of cinnamon tickled the air. Christmas had come along with the cold weather, just like it always did.

Uncle Jim handed me a plate with a cinnamon roll on it. I reclined on the rug by the fire. I was bundled up, my whole family was there, and a mountain of gifts waited for us to open them.

"I can't believe it's so cold today. It really feels like Christmas. It's magic!" I gushed.

Edward snickered. "Only if you call turning up the air-conditioning until your toes freeze magic!"

"What?" I vaulted to my feet, sprinted to the kitchen, and opened the sliding door. A wave of steamy, suffocating air embraced me. I slid the door shut and ran back into the cold living room, staring incredulously at the smiling faces surrounding the Christmas tree.

"Well," I said, popping a bite of warm cinnamon roll into my mouth, "it's magic enough for me!"

 # Comprehension Check

1. Why doesn't the main character in this story want to go to Florida for Christmas?

2. What does Edward do to try to make Florida seem more Christmasy?

3. How do you think Edward really feels about having to entertain his cousin?

4. What makes a holiday like Christmas feel special to you? Why?

# Fishing Lessons

*by Kim T. Griswell*

Hogan's vinyl rain jacket whispered to the gulls and cormorants, "Shush, shush, shush!" They'll scare the fish with all that squawking, Hogan thought. His rowboat rocked against the dock as he set the blue-tipped oars in the locks and shoved them into the water. Jabbing the slate gray water with noisy strokes, he backed toward the middle of the river. His breath fogged the air and fat cold drops of water that flung from the oars splattered his bare hands.

Hogan pointed the boat downriver and dipped the oars deeper. Down, up, pause. Down, up, pause. His shoulder muscles bunched beneath his jacket, toughened by years of rowing. The oars churned the water, ruffling the surface. His father always said the fish could hear him coming a mile away.

When he reached his favorite spot in the shadow of the arched bridge that led into town, Hogan rested his oars in the bottom of the boat and picked up his pole. He sucked in a deep breath to refill his lungs after the exertion. He loved the way the river smelled: the fishy water, the apple-crisp air, the mud banks beneath the reeds and grasses. He tied on his favorite lure, a bright silver minnow, cocked back the pole, released the catch on the reel, and cast the line. The line zipped through the air. The lure hit the water with a satisfying thunk. Now there was nothing to do but wait.

This was the hardest part for Hogan. His mother said that patience was a virtue, but he thought it was a bore. The birds didn't seem patient. The gulls swooped up and down the river, their wings frantic and eyes alert. He could drop a crumb of bread without a gull in sight and look up a second later to see a flock of them careening toward him. The orange-beaked cormorants dove like fighter planes, their wings tucked against their sleek black bodies as they pierced the water.

Action. That's what Hogan liked. Most days he splashed the rowboat up and down the river, flicking his line here and there searching out the best spot, never keeping the lure in one place for more than a few seconds. If it worked for the birds, which were natural fishermen, it should work for him. Still, he seldom caught a fish when his father wasn't with him. When his dad fished, his dad had a natural stillness that attracted fish like metal to a magnet.

Hogan shifted on the hard seat. The rocking boat sent ripples toward the bank. He watched them break against the dank mud. Then he spotted a blue heron. The tall, graceful, blue-gray bird moved so slowly through the reeds along the bank, he hadn't even noticed it. Its toothpick legs took one step at a time, then stopped. Its eyes peered from each side of its head; its long, sharp beak bobbed up and down as it tiptoed through the water. Hogan wondered how it ever managed to catch a fish. It didn't swoop in fast like the gulls or dive-bomb its meals like the cormorants.

Then, almost too fast for Hogan to see, the long beak thrust forward into the murky water. An instant later, it came back up with a tiny silver fish struggling in its grasp. The fish's struggle ended in one quick gulp. Fascinated, Hogan watched as the heron continued its stealthy advance. He sometimes counted almost a minute between one step and the next. Then, just when he thought the big blue-gray bird must have gone to sleep in midstep, that fierce beak would puncture the water again, and another fish would wriggle in its grasp. Hogan started counting under his breath. A fish a minute. That's what the painstaking heron caught. Unbelievable. If he could catch a fish a minute, he'd be a champion.

Okay, he said to himself, today I'm going to be patient. Today I'll be the heron, sliding in like a stealth bomber so quietly the fish won't even know I'm there. He slid the oars back into the locks, then rowed so gently that the water whispered like silk beneath the paddles. He counted a full minute between each stroke, making the boat glide so slowly that its wake was nothing more than the ripple a breeze might make. The current carried him the last few feet toward the spot where he'd seen a fish earlier.

He thumbed the release on the reel gently, muffling the click with his palm. The line spun out silently; the lure dove into the water with barely a sound. Hogan made himself wait, letting the river swim the silver lure with the current. "I am the heron," he whispered. He steadied his elbows on his knees and stuck to the seat like he'd been superglued. Silently, he counted, "One Mississippi, two Mississippi," all the way to 60 seconds before he even dared to breathe.

His neck ached; his shoulder muscles stiffened, but he did not move. Then he felt his line catch. It ducked beneath the surface. He snapped the pole toward him, as quickly as the heron's beak had slashed the water. When he was sure the hook was engaged, he started to reel in the fish. Inch by inch, he tiptoed that fish through the water until he pulled it into the boat. It wriggled on his line, caught securely on the sharp beak of his hook.

"Yes!" Hogan hissed. He would have shouted, but there were more fish to be caught this day. He might not reach the heron's speed of a fish a minute, but now that he'd caught one fish, he knew he could catch another.

 ## Comprehension Check

**1.** Why doesn't Hogan usually catch any fish?

**2.** How is the heron's fishing different from the gulls' and cormorants'?

**3.** Based on the story, why do you think fishing requires stillness and patience?

**4.** What other situations demand patience like fishing?

# Room 142 Meets Mrs. Jones

*by Linda Gondosch*

Lionel Jones could not believe his eyes when the substitute teacher bounced into the room. It was his new stepmother! She gave him a wink as if to say, "For today, let's pretend we don't know each other, okay?" He agreed with a nod.

"Now for attendance," she began. "Frankie Bartello?"

"Present!" called Jeremiah Fink.

"Jeremiah Fink?"

"Present," mumbled Frankie Bartello.

The class mixed up everyone's names until Mrs. Jones called, "Lionel Jones?"

"Present!" said Lionel and Alexander Peppersmith.

"You can't both be Lionel," said Mrs. Jones.

"I'm Lionel," said Lionel, as if she didn't already know!

As the reading lesson began, Jeremiah Fink twisted a paper clip, stuck it beneath his desk lid, and twanged it with his thumb. On hearing the vibrating noise, the substitute glanced up from her book. Soon, 15 thumbs twanged paper clips; strange boing, boing sounds echoed throughout Room 142.

Mrs. Jones ran to the telephone. "I need the custodian here immediately. Hurry, I think the radiator is about to explode!"

Lionel dropped his box of paper clips onto the floor. When his stepmother saw the paper clips and noticed Jeremiah Fink twanging one, she said, "Never mind. Cancel the custodian."

At recess everyone gathered around Lionel. "What's with you, Lionel?" demanded Jeremiah. "Don't you want to drive the sub crazy?"

"Just follow the rest of us," said Consuelo Valdez.

"Better yet, you be the leader," Frankie Bartello said as his lip curled menacingly. "When we go back, take the boa constrictor out of the tank and hide it in the teacher's desk. That will get her." He belly laughed and slapped Lionel on the back.

"Oooo!" taunted several classmates.

What a fix! Lionel tried not to meet anyone's questioning gaze. Frankie had just handed him the perfect way to get even with his new stepmother. After all, he never wanted a stepmother in the first place, but a snake in her drawer? She was petrified of snakes.

They poured back into Room 142. While his stepmother wrote on the chalkboard, Lionel scooped up the snake with a stick. He tiptoed to the teacher's desk, but suddenly stopped when he remembered the cookies she had baked the day before: chocolate chip with coconut, his favorite. As he stood there indecisively, the snake slithered out of his hand, down his leg, and onto the floor. Before he could grab it, the boa escaped across the room and out the door.

Mrs. Jones turned around just in time to catch sight of its tail disappearing out the door.

"What was that?" She grabbed the back of her chair to steady herself.

"Our snake!" hollered Jeremiah. "He's loose!"

Mrs. Jones chased the snake down the hallway with the class right behind her. She dove for the snake as it slithered around the corner, catching it with both hands.

"Wow!" said Frankie. "She's brave."

"She didn't yell at us or anything," said Consuelo.

"Let's stop the tricks," said Jeremiah.

Lionel smiled. "Yeah, let's treat the sub as if she were," he hesitated, "our very own mother!"

"Or grandmother," said Jeremiah.

"Or big sister," said Consuelo.

Everyone returned to their desks and sat quietly. Lionel couldn't remember the class ever being so well behaved. Mrs. Jones put the snake in the tank and began the spelling test.

After the test, she passed out chocolate chip and coconut cookies. "Because you are such a good class," she said with a wink toward Lionel.

 ## Comprehension Check

**1.** Why doesn't Lionel want to drive the sub crazy like the rest of the class?

**2.** How do you think Lionel feels about his new stepmother. Why?

**3.** Do you think Lionel would have put the snake in the desk drawer if it had not crawled away? Why or why not?

**4.** What would you do if a relative substituted for your teacher?

# Recount

*by Kim T. Griswell*

Morgan stuffed her hands in the front pockets of her cargo pants to keep from biting her nails. Followed by her campaign manager, Nancy Austin, she made her way to the principal's office. Dr. Ramsey invited her in.

"Nancy, you can wait out here with Kevin's campaign manager, Bob." She motioned to a line of wooden chairs in the outer office.

Morgan's opponent in the race for class president slumped in a cushioned chair in front of Dr. Ramsey's desk. The principal tapped a pencil on her desktop and looked over the top of her reading glasses at the two candidates.

"I know you're both wondering why you've been called into my office. I'm afraid we have a problem with the votes from your class election."

Morgan's back stiffened. "What do you mean? The votes were counted yesterday. I won by four votes."

Dr. Ramsey dropped her pencil into a soup-can pencil holder. "There's some question as to the accuracy of the count," she said.

The butterflies that had flown from Morgan's stomach when the last vote was counted returned. This time they weren't floating; they were doing the backstroke.

"All right!" Kevin sat up straighter.

"But I don't understand. What happened?" Morgan's hands found their way out of her pockets, and she sat on them. Nail chewing did not show confidence.

"Your teacher found five votes that had 'fallen' behind her desk. She doesn't know how they got there, but since you won by such a small margin, they will have to be counted."

Kevin looked at Morgan like she'd suddenly grown antlers. Did he think she was responsible for the uncounted votes?

When Dr. Ramsey dismissed them, Kevin shouldered his way past Morgan, almost knocking her against the door frame.

"I knew you couldn't have won fairly," he said as he glared at her.

Morgan clenched her fists. "I did not cheat, Kevin Bradley!"

Back in their classroom, Nancy and Morgan stood at one end of the table; Kevin and Bob slouched at the other. Miss Trimble tallied the votes on the white board for a second time. The candidates and their campaign managers supervised the process. Soon the dizzying smell of red and green dry-erase markers made the butterflies in Morgan's stomach begin to swim upside down.

She leaned toward Nancy. "Keep an eye on those two," she whispered. "I've got to get some fresh air, but I'll be right back."

When she returned, the count was complete. Bob had ventured from his spot beside Kevin and now rested a shoulder against the white board. "Well, well," he said. "Looks like your little attempt to win failed."

"We didn't hide those votes!" Morgan put her hands on her hips and stood her ground.

"Either way," Kevin grinned, "the votes have been recounted. You lose."

Her lips tightened into a straight line as she stared at the red and green marks. There were six more red tally marks than there were green marks. She had lost by six votes. How was that possible? She turned to Miss Trimble.

"Do you remember yesterday's results?" she asked.

Miss Trimble nodded. "You won by four votes."

"And today she lost by six." Nancy shook her head. "That's impossible. Even if all five of the new votes were for Kevin, he would have won by only a single vote."

Miss Trimble looked from one student to the other. Morgan scrutinized Bob, who was propped against the white board as if guarding it. Oh, how she would like to wipe that smirk off his face.

"Nancy's right," Morgan said. "It doesn't add up."

Bob stepped away from the board and stood next to Morgan. "Are you questioning Miss Trimble's tally?"

Morgan turned toward him. "Of course not, I'm—" She stopped and stared at the sleeve of Bob's white sweatshirt.

"What? What are you staring at?" Bob looked down nervously.

"That!" Morgan pointed to green smudges covering the sleeve of his shirt.

"Uh, how did those get there?" he mumbled, pulling his sleeve out and trying to brush away the smudges.

"Maybe when you wiped off a row of green marks!" Morgan said.

"Bob! How could you?" Kevin thumped his campaign manager on the shoulder. "Miss Trimble, I assure you I had nothing to do with this."

Bob glared. "Oh, sure. Just like you had nothing to do with knocking those votes off the desk yesterday just after Nancy and her buddies voted."

Kevin's gaze dropped to the toes of his running shoes. "All's well that ends well, right?"

"No, Kevin," said Miss Trimble. "All is well because your classmates get to have the president they voted for."

 ## Comprehension Check

1. Why does the vote for class president have to be recounted?

2. How do you think the two candidates feel about one another? Why?

3. How does Morgan know that something is wrong with the second count?

4. Do you think the other students in the class should be told about the recount, or do you think it should be kept between the candidates, Miss Trimble, and Dr. Ramsey?

# Encore!

*by Kim Childress*

The butterflies fluttered madly. Casey closed her eyes, took a deep breath, and visualized herself at the piano. Another deep breath, and she began imagining her fingers flying over the keys, perfectly hitting every note.

The cacophony of tuning instruments brought her back to reality. Her teacher, Mrs. Ornacle, helped Casey's older brother Roger organize his sheet music. He'd been clowning around and had knocked it off his stand. On stage, the microphone screeched. The recital had started.

Roger adjusted his stand and continued practicing his viola, moving his bow back and forth. He seemed unflappable, as if the audience waiting in the shadows beyond the stage did not exist. But this was Roger's third recital; it was Casey's first.

To calm herself, Casey pictured her mother playing, making the piano sound high and fast, like a bird's song, or slow and deep, like an ocean tide. Casey wanted to play like that.

The song she would play tonight was her favorite. It reminded her of the ocean. Low chords quickly climbed up the scale, building into booming thunder and crashing waves. The piece was fast, loud, and fun to play. It had three pages with one page turn. The turn came right as the chord progression moved up an octave, and Casey's fingers sometimes botched their way to the higher keys. Anxious to perfect the piece, she had worked for weeks getting ready.

On stage, Mrs. Ornacle gave Casey's introduction. It was time.

Casey crossed the stage and took her place at the piano, trying not to notice the packed auditorium. She set her songbook on the piano, and it fell open to the page. As the audience grew silent, Casey became aware of a ringing in her ears.

She took a deep breath, whispered "Relax," and began. She missed a note immediately, but kept going. Her heart raced and her fingers picked up the tempo, playing faster than the music was supposed to be played.

Casey knew most of the notes by heart. Her right hand started playing ahead of her left. Trying to regain the pace, she looked at her hands. When she looked back up, she couldn't find her place. In a panic, Casey slammed her hands down on the keys and ran off the stage.

Immediately, Mrs. Ornacle stood beside her. Casey saw the other kids staring at her. Someone snickered, and Mrs. Ornacle hissed, "Shush!"

"I blew it!" Casey cried. "I messed up in front of everyone!"

"Casey," Mrs. Ornacle said firmly, "you need to go back out and finish."

"No way!" Casey gasped. "They'll laugh at me!"

"They won't," Mrs. Ornacle said. "I know you can play that piece. You know it too. Which would be worse: leaving without finishing or facing the audience again?"

Casey couldn't decide.

"Look at it this way," Mrs. Ornacle winked. "You couldn't play much worse."

Casey smiled despite her tears. She wiped her face with the sleeve of her new dress. Before thinking about it anymore, she walked back onstage, her heart thumping almost loudly enough to drown out the murmuring audience. Almost.

She began again. Just like practice, she thought, and slowly counted in her head: one, two, three, four. It was working! Her fingers felt looser. Whoops! She hit a B note instead of a C. She flinched at the sound but continued.

Playing loudly, forcefully, Casey made it to the second page. The turn was coming. Keeping her eyes on the music, she kept the tune going with her left hand while she reached up with her right. She turned the page, glancing down at the keyboard for just a moment. Long enough! She skipped an entire line.

Casey played louder, building for the crescendo. She pictured the storm ending and the waves gently rolling, but instead of tapering off for the diminuendo, her fingers banged out the last notes.

Finally it was over. Scattered applause filled the auditorium. Casey ran offstage to the practice room and sat at the piano. Her hands shook wildly. A knock at the door made her jump. Without waiting for her to answer, Roger pushed open the door and stepped inside.

"You played horribly," he said.

Casey felt a flush of anger creep up her neck.

"I can't believe you went back out." He looked down at his feet. "I don't think I could have. You may not have the fingering of a master yet, but you've sure got the nerve!"

Casey sat speechless.

"I'm almost up." He glanced at her face, then looked away. "I gotta go." He smiled and hurried off.

Casey sighed deeply. No matter what the other kids said, she had finished. She closed her eyes and pictured herself at next year's recital. She could see it—a perfect performance, the audience shouting, "Encore!"

Smiling, Casey got up and returned to hear the rest of the recital. "Next year," she whispered. "Next year."

 ## Comprehension Check

**1.** Why is Casey nervous about the recital?

**2.** How do you think Casey feels when she runs offstage?

**3.** After the performance, Roger says that Casey has the nerve of a master. What do you think he means?

**4.** Some people think that it takes talent to become a musician. Some think it takes skill. What do you think it takes to become a musician?

# Savings Plan

*by Rusty Fischer*

Kendall Jackson was tired after yet another long day of mowing lawns in the brutal July sun. While all of his friends were out enjoying summer, Kendall was stuck mowing lawns to make extra money. Each night after work, Kendall rushed home and dove under his bed to stow the handful of dollar bills he had made that day. He stuffed them inside the shoebox that he liked to call his "safe."

He dragged himself over to the calendar hanging crookedly over his desk. Crossing off yet another day in red marker, he murmured to himself, "Only six more days until Mom's birthday."

After another long week of mowing lawns, Kendall muttered, "I can't believe tomorrow is Mom's birthday!"

Finally, he could quit mowing lawns and start enjoying his summer. Consulting his bulging safe, Kendall counted his money and could barely believe it. He had managed to save just over $100.

"So, are you excited, Mom?" he asked that night at dinner.

"About what?" she asked.

"You know, tomorrow's your birthday," Kendall reminded her. "What do you want?"

"Oh, just for everyone to be safe and sound for another year." Kendall's mom smiled at his rolling eyes. "Okay, okay," she admitted. "I can't deny that I've had my eye on that fancy new coffeemaker down at the mall. But it's way too expensive."

That night Kendall slept soundly, knowing that he wouldn't have to get up at the crack of dawn to mow lawns. Lazily, he woke up late and took a shower before jumping into shorts, a T-shirt, and his battered, grass-stained sneakers.

He would have said happy birthday to his mom, but at this late hour, she would already be waiting tables at the diner.

Oh, well, he thought, leaping onto his bike, at least when she gets home tonight, she'll be surprised when she sees her brand-new coffeemaker!

Kendall pumped his legs all the way to the mall, slowing down only when he arrived at the bustling parking lot. He leapt off his bike and locked it up tight before racing inside to the gourmet store.

As he passed a shoe-store window, something caught his eye. A pair of cool red Nike® running shoes gleamed in the display window. Glancing down at his beat-up sneakers, Kendall could not resist stepping inside the store to see how much they cost. Kendall whistled as he looked at the sticker on the sole of the shoe—$90. He knew that if he bought these shoes, he wouldn't be able to get his mom the coffeemaker she wanted. He glanced down at his grass-stained shoes one more time. Maybe they had a cheaper coffeemaker he could buy.

Cycling home, Kendall could hardly contain himself. The new shoes on his feet were so much better than his old ones.

When he got home, he couldn't wait to show them to his mom.

"Oh, my," she said. She didn't smile like he had expected. Instead, she looked down at her hands, up at the television set, everywhere but at Kendall. "Those certainly are nice shoes. Since you bought them for yourself, I guess my birthday present is not having to buy them for you when you go back to school."

Kendall had almost forgotten the box behind his back. "Happy birthday!" he said to his mom as he held out the new coffeemaker.

His mother hugged him. "You didn't forget me after all. When I saw you come through the door in those new shoes, I just assumed you'd spent all of your lawn-mowing money on yourself."

Kendall looked down at his new shoes. "I almost did," he admitted. "The new Nike shoes had just come out, and I was all ready to buy them. But then I remembered how much you enjoy your nightly cup of coffee. So I ran out of the store before I did something stupid and bought your coffeemaker instead."

"Then how did you buy the shoes?" His mom's brow creased.

"The coffeemaker was on sale!" Kendall explained. "That left me just enough money to buy this pair of shoes."

"Come here." His mom held out her arms for a hug.

Kendall blushed as his mom hugged him again. "Happy birthday," he whispered in her ear. "Now let's cut that cake. I've got to get up early and mow a lot more lawns before I can afford those Nike shoes I want!"

 **Comprehension Check**

**1.** Why is Kendall working so hard over the summer break?

**2.** How do you think Kendall feels about his mother?

**3.** Do you think Kendall will earn enough money to get the shoes he really wants? Why or why not?

**4.** Describe a time when you have done without something you wanted so that someone else could have something special.

# Sound the Alarm!

*by Kim T. Griswell*

The call came at 1:15 A.M. Owen fidgeted restlessly, pulled the covers up tighter around his neck, and tucked his knees toward his chest. He was used to middle-of-the-night calls. Since his father had been elected sheriff of Harbor Side two years earlier, they'd averaged three night calls per week. Owen had learned to gauge the seriousness of the calls by the tone of his father's voice. After a few seconds, he realized that this one was pretty serious.

Owen sat up in bed, listening.

"What do you mean, Hattie?" His father's voice had a higher tone than usual, edgy.

"Yes. All right. I'll wake up Ralph and get him down to the fire station immediately."

Ralph Anderson was the fire chief. This really was serious.

Owen hopped out of bed. The bare wood floor felt cold enough to form ice on his feet, so he shoved them into his unlaced sneakers.

"Anything I can do?" He stuck his head out the door. Since his mom died, he and his dad had looked out for each other. If his dad needed help, Owen did whatever he could.

His father rushed past, headed for his own room. As he dressed, Owen stood shivering by the door. "An earthquake just hit Alaska. They've issued a tsunami warning for the coast."

Owen tensed. "You mean we might get hit by a tidal wave?"

His dad frowned, then nodded.

"I've already called Ralph. He's heading down to the station to sound the alarm."

Owen felt the cold from his feet creeping all the way up his body. Living on the coast, he knew a lot about tsunamis. He'd read all about the tsunami that wiped out a large part of Crescent City, California, in 1964.

His dad put a hand on Owen's shoulder. "Just stay calm," he said. "Everything will be fine. Ralph will have that siren going any minute now." He bent down to look Owen in the eye. "You won't be in any danger here. We're far enough up the hill that no wave can possibly reach us."

"But what about you?" He grabbed his dad's sleeve. "You can't go into town! It's only ten feet above sea level!"

His dad clasped the hand on his sleeve. "I won't take any chances, Owen, but right now, the town needs me more than you do. There'll be scared, sleepy folks down there. And scared, sleepy folks get disoriented. They need someone with a cool head to make sure they get to safety."

He finished putting on his coat and gave Owen a salute. "Hold down the fort till I return."

Owen tried not to think about what might be happening downtown as he listened for the warning siren. When no earsplitting howl tore the air, Owen began to really worry. If the siren didn't sound and a tsunami hit—

Owen didn't want to imagine what might happen, but his mind kept showing him pictures like the ones he'd seen of Crescent City: houses swept from their foundations and deposited five blocks away; shops bursting apart as if they'd been bombed; cars, logs, doors, parts of boats—all mixed together and stacked up like some kid's rejected toys. People had died in Crescent City, because back then, they had no early-warning system.

Owen stared out the front window. The fire station was only a few blocks downhill from his house and he could see that there were no lights on in the building. Wiping the devastating pictures of Crescent City from his mind, he started tying his sneakers. If a tsunami was coming, there wasn't time to wait for the fire chief. Someone had to sound the alarm.

As he dashed to the back door and burst into the night, a sense of urgency overtook him. His feet skidded on the gravel drive, but he kept going. He hit Sixth Street running and didn't stop until he reached the door of the fire station. By then, his chest felt as if he should turn the fire hose on it. He grabbed the doorknob and turned.

It was locked. Now what? No one was in the streets nearby. His dad was somewhere downtown, right where the wave would hit, and it could happen any time now. Owen wanted nothing more than to go home and slink beneath his covers. He was no hero; he was scared out of his mind.

As his breathing slowed, his father's words came back to him: "Scared, sleepy folks get disoriented. They need someone with a cool head to make sure they get to safety."

"Pull yourself together, Owen," he whispered. "Take a deep breath. Think."

He looked around and spotted some rocks encircling the flagpole. Grabbing the biggest one, he stepped a few feet away from the window in the door, took aim, and heaved it as hard as he could. The fact that he was breaking and entering didn't bother him at all; right now, all that mattered was getting inside the building. The tinkle of shattering glass was followed by the angry howl of a burglar alarm.

Good, Owen thought, that'll wake up folks close by. He reached over the broken glass and felt inside for the doorknob; with a quick turn, he was in. He'd had the tour of the firehouse enough times to know just where to go. He raced down the main hallway and into the fire chief's office, flipped on the lights, and then jabbed the red button on the alarm.

The alarm wailed so loudly that Owen had to cover his ears, but the grin spreading across his face reflected his relief. He raced back outside. All around him, lights came on. Soon people began to stumble out of their houses—scared, sleepy, and disoriented.

"What's going on?" an elderly man yelled from the yard across the street.

"Tsunami!" Owen yelled back. "Head up the hill as quick as you can!"

Owen thought about his dad hurrying through town, being strong and calm, lending a hand, making sure everyone got out in time. But would he get out?

A crowd gathered on the hillside near Owen's house. Each minute felt like an hour, so that soon, he could no longer tell how much time had elapsed. As people streamed up the hill, Owen heard a sound coming from the sea that froze his breath in his chest: A sucking sound like that of a great vacuum cleaner filled the night. For a moment, the world seemed to hold its breath; then the ocean began to roar. Tsunami!

Owen bent over, clutching his knees; tears welled up in his eyes. The roaring sound increased until it pounded in his ears, but he still hadn't seen his father come up the hill. His stomach began to churn, and he wondered if he was going to be sick.

He watched mutely as the wave smashed into the shops along Harbor Drive. The town went black as power lines sparked and fell. Overhead, the full moon illuminated the wave that rushed forward. It pushed debris in its path as it devoured Front Street and then Holladay Drive, spitting out the remains of homes and businesses when it hit Third.

"Dad," Owen whispered. All the air went out of his lungs, as if the wave had slammed into his chest. His legs began to wobble.

Then someone grabbed him. Owen looked up.

"Dad!" he shouted, throwing himself at his father. "I thought..."

"It's okay, son. I'm here." His father's voice was deep, filled with fatigue and relief.

Owen turned back toward town. The wave had receded to the harbor, sucking the

skeletons of the few buildings still standing into the sea.

"Did everyone get out?"

His dad shook his head. "I don't know." He turned to Chief Anderson, who had just jogged up beside him. "Until that siren sounded, Ralph, I thought we were going to lose everyone from here to the waterfront. Most of them are safe because of you."

Ralph shook his head. "Don't thank me," he said. "I just got here!"

"What?" Owen's dad turned back to him.

Owen looked down at his sneakers.

His dad put an arm around Owen's shoulder and gripped it tightly. "Thanks for keeping a cool head, son."

 # Comprehension Check

**1.** What is another name for a tsunami?

**2.** Why does Owen's father go into town despite the possible danger?

**3.** What personality trait or traits enable Owen to help his father and the rest of the town?

**4.** The story never mentions why the fire chief, Ralph Anderson, does not sound the alarm. What might have kept him from doing so?

# The Great Chocolate Caper

*by Rusty Fischer*

Darwina Edison Carver, Winny for short, fancied herself a pint-sized private eye. She loved mysteries and had read all of Sherlock Holmes's adventures. Secretly, she considered herself the greatest junior detective this side of Holmes himself.

Of course, she didn't always get a chance to show off her great detective skills. Most unsolved mysteries at Madison Elementary School were of the missing milk money variety, easily solved by discovering that the "victim" had a hole in his pocket!

One day, however, Winny was able to use all of her detecting skills, and then some! Mr. Richards, her fifth-grade teacher, had a special announcement that morning.

"Class," he said, "this afternoon we are having a surprise guest."

"Who is it?" asked the curious class. "Who is it?"

"Well," Mr. Richards smiled. "Our very special guest is none other than Mr. Chocolate himself, Carlton Cocoa!"

Winny could hardly believe it. Carlton Cocoa was the owner, head chef, and mastermind behind the local chocolate maker, The Cocoa Company. Mr. Richards finally got the class to settle down enough to explain that, in honor of their very special guest's 20th year in business, he had ordered a very special welcome present.

Everyone watched as the school janitor, Mr. Tidy, wheeled the present in from the hall on a squeaky cart. Mr. Richards hefted a giant chocolate bar onto his desk. Everyone crowded close as he wrote "Congratulations!" on the bar with vanilla frosting. Needless to say, it was another few minutes before the class quieted down enough for Mr. Richards to take them out for recess. Mr. Tidy followed them out of the room and locked the door behind him before returning to work.

When the students returned to their room, however, they noticed instantly that something was wrong. A rather large bite was missing from the chocolate bar!

"Oh, no!" cried Mr. Richards. "Who would do such a thing?"

Spying a stack of Styrofoam® plates next to the giant chocolate bar, Winny raised her hand.

"I think I know how to find out," she said.

She remembered a great mystery in which one of her favorite detectives took bite impressions from several suspects and used them to solve a crime. Winny wrote each student's name on one of the Styrofoam plates. Then she instructed each student to bite softly into the plate with his or her name written on it. As Mr. Richards observed, Winny carefully compared the bite marks on the plates with those on the corner of the chocolate bar.

As the class members eyed each other suspiciously, Winny announced her conclusion.

"I am proud to say that no one in this class took a bite out of the chocolate bar." Everyone cheered.

Mr. Richards quieted the class and asked, "Then who, Winny? Who took a bite out of the candy bar?"

Winny frowned. The classroom door had been locked when they left for recess. No one could have entered the classroom after they left the room. So who could have taken that bite? Just then, Winny heard the sound of squeaky wheels outside in the hall. That's it! She snapped her fingers, grabbed a Styrofoam plate, and ran into the hall.

Moments later, everyone pushed close to watch Winny compare a new set of bite marks with those in the candy bar. A perfect match!

"Winny! You found the culprit!" Mr. Richards beamed. "How?"

"Elementary, my dear Mr. Richards." She winked. "When I heard wheels squeaking in the hallway a minute ago, I remembered that there was someone else in the class-

room before we left for recess. In fact, that someone was the last one to leave the room!"

"Who? Who was it?" Everyone wanted to know.

"Mr. Tidy!" Winny announced.

"Excellent observation, Winny," said Mr. Richards. "I'll deal with Mr. Tidy after our special guest has come and gone. Until then, how do I solve the not-so-tiny matter of a bite mark in our welcome present?"

Asking for permission first, Winny took the cake server with which Mr. Richards had intended to slice up the chocolate bar. Very carefully, she cut around the edge of the bite mark. Unfortunately, this lopped off the last few letters of "Congratulations!"

Spying the vanilla frosting with which Mr. Richards had written his message, Winny went to work. First, she lopped off more chocolate to even up the sides of the bar. Then she wrote words above and below the old message. When she was through, the new message said, "Our Class Congratulates You!"

"Perfect!" said Mr. Richards. "But what are we supposed to do with all of this extra chocolate? I have to get rid of it before Mr. Cocoa gets here, and he could show up at any minute."

For once, Mr. Richards had no problem finding volunteers!

 **Comprehension Check**

**1.** Who is Winny's favorite detective?

**2.** Why do you think the students are so excited about their special guest?

**3.** What clues lead Winny to the person who took the bite out of the chocolate?

**4.** If you were Mr. Richards, how would you deal with Mr. Tidy?

# The Haunted Lighthouse

*by Kim T. Griswell*

The moment Carey stepped into the dimly lit parlor of the salt-scented house that formed the base of the Crescent City lighthouse, a shadow passed over her and a chill settled between her shoulder blades. She chalked it up to the cold wind blowing off the Pacific and the icy fog that surrounded the lighthouse like a shroud.

The lighthouse keeper had just raised her arm, starting to motion the tour group to follow her up the stairs, but she hesitated. Carey felt the cold deepening, as if the fog outside had entered by a hatch in the roof and now flowed like an icy waterfall down the stairs toward her. The hair on her arms bristled, and she felt an overwhelming desire to run. She wasn't the only one to notice. A little boy suddenly ducked beneath his mother's raincoat. A long-haired teen fidgeted with his ponytail, pulling it away from the back of his neck as if a spider were tickling his skin. One by one, each person stepped back, looked over his shoulder, or shuddered as something unseen passed from the stairs into the hallway, then moved toward the parlor.

The keeper sighed. "Ladies and gentlemen, you've just had the dubious pleasure of encountering one of our most infamous residents. One whom, I'm sorry to say, I never had the chance to meet while he lived, but whom I have encountered almost daily since coming to live in this house."

The tourists glanced around nervously, as if expecting the specter to emerge from hiding, but nothing appeared.

"Shall we proceed?" Once more the keeper held out her hand, but now the group milling about in the parlor hesitated. Unspoken questions went from eye to eye. Finally, Carey stepped forward. "If your spooky houseguest has just come downstairs, then I'm all for going up."

Nervous laughter eased the tension as, one by one, the others followed Carey's lead. The narrow, wooden stairway zigzagged back and forth up to one landing, then another. The keeper stopped at the second landing. Carey peered through a skinny door into a closet-sized room. A rough-hewn wooden chest covered with a lace cloth rested at the foot of an uncomfortable-looking twin bed. Atop the cloth sat a box carved from redwood. Though the wood shone with many polishings, its bright surface was marred by droplets of water beaded on its lid in an odd fingertip pattern.

"Looks as if our visitor stopped by to check on his things before coming downstairs to join us," the keeper said.

Carey didn't like the way she said "join us." She glanced over her shoulder. No shadowy figure lurked among the tourists.

"The contents of this box are all that is left of the earthly possessions of one Samuel J. DeWolf, the captain of the *Brother Jonathan*, a ship that sank near the shore one storm-tossed afternoon in 1865."

She lifted the lid and waved her hand over the box. "A rusted straight razor, the tattered remains of a leather-bound journal, and a gold pocket watch engraved with his name."

Carey peered into the box. She wasn't sure how the lighthouse keeper knew the watch belonged to Captain DeWolf. The letters on the back of the watch looked like chicken scratches. No matter how she squinted, she couldn't read them.

"'Twas greed that sank the *Jonathan*." The keeper winked. "She was loaded

down with more freight than she was designed to carry. They packed on an ore crusher that weighed several tons, more barrels of butter than you could shake a stick at, and a cache of gold coins for a treaty payment." She winked at Carey. "And, some say, a private company piled her full of crates filled to the top with 20-dollar gold pieces."

Someone behind Carey whistled.

"Captain DeWolf told the company's agent to stop taking on cargo. The ship was too deep in the water. The agent told DeWolf that if he didn't take her out, they'd find another captain who would. Then he went back to filling her hold." The keeper shook her head and stared at the box for a few seconds, then clicked it shut. "Since DeWolf knew the ship better than anyone else, he must have figured that his passengers would be safer with him than another captain."

She stepped out of the little room, scooting the tourists onto the landing. "They tried to leave San Francisco around noon on July 28," she snorted, "but the boat was so overloaded, she was stuck in the mud. It took high tide and a tugboat to get her out of the harbor."

"So what happened? Did the ship sink?" the ponytailed teenager prompted.

The keeper nodded. She motioned for them to follow her to the next landing, then up a narrow, winding metal staircase to the tower that housed the beacon. They stepped out onto a narrow walkway guarded by a brass rail that encircled the light. Carey stared out across the sea. Waves burst against the black rocks surrounding the island. "See that speck out there?"

"I see it!" The little boy who'd been hiding behind his mother jumped up and down, pointing. Carey shaded her eyes and followed the line of his finger.

"Yep. That's Seal Rock. By the time the *Brother Jonathan* reached Crescent City, a storm was brewing. DeWolf made it out past St. George's Reef, then decided to turn back, wait it out in the safety of the harbor. After they passed Seal Rock there," she pointed toward the black spike on the horizon, "he charted a course that should have been free of obstructions."

She turned her back on the sea and leaned against the rail. "Unfortunately, the charts he had weren't very accurate. A wave heaved that ship up and dropped it smack dab atop a rock that rose from the ocean bottom. Jonathan Rock they call it now."

"Captain DeWolf?" Carey asked.

The keeper shook her head. "Went down with the ship. Only 19 out of 244 people survived that sinking. And all because of greed."

Led by the keeper, Carey followed the other tourists back down the stairs and into the foyer. At the bottom of the stairs, she stopped to glance at a framed black-and-white photo hanging just to the right of the front door. A haunted-looking gentleman with a full beard and mustache stared back at her. A brass plate screwed into the frame bore the inscription "Captain Samuel J. DeWolf." The chill Carey had felt earlier crept down her spine again, but she shrugged it off. It was time to leave the tragedies of the lighthouse behind.

She opened the front door and stepped into a brisk wind blowing in from the Pacific. Overhead, a seagull screeched, bobbing and dipping in the wind currents. The lighthouse keeper told a good ghost story, Carey thought. Too bad it was nothing but a tale to make the tour more interesting. As she started down the rock-strewn trail toward the shore, a shadow passed over the sun and the chill between her shoulders deepened once more. She had the strange feeling that someone was watching her. She turned slowly back toward the lighthouse, then froze.

The picture window in the front parlor was fogged over, as if blown by icy breath. Across the window, in a shaky script, were written the words "Tell them if they had not overloaded us, this would never have happened."

 ## Comprehension Check

1. Why does the lighthouse keeper think the ghost of Captain DeWolf haunts the lighthouse?

2. The lighthouse keeper claims that greed caused the sinking of the *Brother Jonathan*. Why do you think she believes that?

3. What clues does the story give as to what might have caused the *Brother Jonathan* to sink?

4. What might Captain DeWolf have done to prevent the sinking of the *Brother Jonathan*?

# Red Water Rescue

*by Kim T. Griswell*

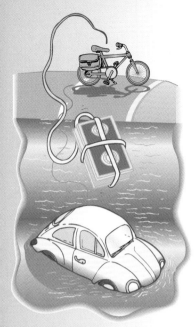

Clouds bubbled over the mountains like whipped cream on hot chocolate. Chloe could almost taste them. She shifted her bike into low gear and slowed as her tires skidded on wet gravel. It had rained for three days straight. She'd decided to take advantage of the lull between storms to return a video that was two days overdue.

"You be careful," her mother had warned. "Weatherman says it's still storming up on Grandfather Mountain. There's a flash flood watch in effect for the valley."

Chloe was so glad to be out of the house after being stuck inside for three days that she didn't care what the forecast said. She had planned to spend the weekend camping. Her bike pack was filled with gear the rain had kept her from using. Instead, she'd been forced to stay inside and watch the same video over and over until she could recite each character's lines by heart.

After cycling across the highway, Chloe turned toward town. As she churned up the last hill, she noticed an unusual sound, like water running in a toilet bowl, but much louder. Then she crested the hill and skidded to a halt.

Water flowed across the street at the bottom of the hill—thick, red-clay water that billowed like silk.

"Now what?" Chloe glanced back over her shoulder. She already owed two days in late charges and another day would eat up the rest of her allowance. Chloe descended the hill, edging her bike closer to the rippling water. It didn't look very deep, so it couldn't be dangerous. With a running start, she'd have no trouble crossing the stream.

As Chloe mounted her bike, she heard a car approaching. Its engine snuffled like it had a cold. Chloe grinned. It could only be Ms. Calihan, the town librarian, in her lemonade yellow Volkswagen® Beetle®. Ms. Calihan waved cheerily as she passed. Chloe waved back. The car hesitated as it neared the mud-red stream. Then Ms. Calihan gunned the engine and scooted forward. Chloe watched as water swirled around the car's tires, then over its bumper. She gripped the handlebars of her bike.

"Man, that's a lot deeper than I thought." She watched the car inch forward, then stop.

"Come on," Ms. Calihan urged, but the snuffling little car gave one last sneeze and died.

The water kept rising. Chloe held her breath, waiting for Ms. Calihan to get out of the car. She popped the door open, but the rippling red water slammed it shut. Had the water been up to the door a second ago? Chloe didn't think so. Ms. Calihan opened the door again; the water closed it. Chloe eased her bike to the ground and hurried forward.

At the edge of the rushing water, she cupped her hands around her mouth and yelled, "Try the other door!"

Ms. Calihan glanced into the rearview mirror; her forehead wrinkled with worry and her tiny blue eyes filled with fear. She gestured toward her ears and shrugged.

The water no longer sounded like a toilet running. Now, it sounded like a waterfall. Ms. Calihan couldn't hear her. Chloe pointed to the door on the other side of the car.

Ms. Calihan nodded, scooted across the seat, and then shoved open the door. This time, she wasn't fighting against the current. The door opened, but water immediately flooded the car. It began to lift and wobble like a helium balloon struggling against a string. Ms. Calihan hesitated as she scrutinized the angry red water, then looked up at Chloe. If the water was strong enough to move the car, Chloe realized, it could sweep the librarian downstream.

As the car began to drift, Chloe knew she had to act. Rope, she thought, I have to find rope. Then she remembered the camping gear in her pack. She tore into the pack and yanked out a coil of rope. Tying one end of the rope to the nearest tree, Chloe ventured back to the water's edge.

"Get ready!" she called. Ms. Calihan turned sideways in the seat and nodded. Chloe took aim at the librarian's hands and threw the rope. It fell limply into the water, yards away from the car. The raging water grabbed it and pulled it downstream. Chloe quickly reeled it back in. She needed something to weigh it down, but what? Then she remembered the video cassette.

"Hang on!" she called, then raced back to her bike. She tied the rope onto the cassette like she was tying up a Christmas package, then yanked the knot tight.

"Okay!" This time, Ms. Calihan turned sideways and put her feet in the water. Chloe swung the tape out to her side, once, twice, three times, winding it up like a lasso. Then she threw, holding her breath; even with the tape weighing it down, there was no guarantee the rope would reach. Chloe vaulted into the air when Ms. Calihan caught the video, clinging to it like it was the last life jacket on the *Titanic*.

"You can get out of the car now!" Chloe called. "Just hang on to the rope and try to stay on your feet."

Little by little, Ms. Calihan inched along the rope. At last, she stumbled out of the treacherous water. She bent forward; her chest heaved as she fought for breath. Chloe ran to her.

"Are you okay?" she put a hand on Ms. Calihan's back.

The librarian nodded. "Yes." She gave Chloe a shaky grin. "And you, young lady, will never get another library fine as long as you live!"

Chloe held up the soggy cassette dangling from the rope. "That's good," she said with a laugh, " 'cause I'm going to need all my money to pay for this video!"

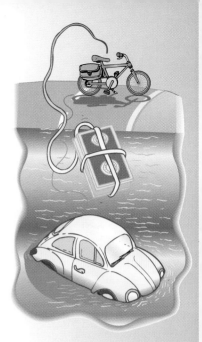

---

 ## Comprehension Check

**1.** What clues does the story give that Chloe might encounter a flash flood?

**2.** What might have happened to Chloe if she had bicycled through the water as she'd planned?

**3.** How does Chloe save Ms. Calihan from the flood?

**4.** Do you think Chloe will have to pay for the damaged video? Why or why not?

# The Treasure

*by Linda C. Fiedler*

"I can't believe you talked me into this," signed Meg.

Laura grinned. "We have to find the treasure before Mom turns this place into an inn, don't we?"

"I guess," signed Meg.

Laura pumped her bike along the oak-lined drive leading to the faded pre–Civil War mansion. Meg followed reluctantly. Though her sister, Laura, had been deaf since birth, she never let her disability put the brakes on her ravenous curiosity. To Laura, finding a lost treasure was like a triple-scoop ice-cream sundae just waiting to be eaten.

On the front porch, Meg grabbed Laura's arm, signing, "This place has been boarded up for years. People have tried before and didn't find a thing!"

Annoyed, Laura signed, "All those family stories about a treasure hidden in the house can't be wrong. Plenty of Southerners hid valuables from the Northern troops. Money, jewels, silverware—who knows what we'll find."

After unlocking the door, Laura squeezed through the boards blocking the entrance. When Meg hesitated, Laura motioned her forward. She pointed to their flashlights, then flipped hers on. Meg followed suit. The dim circles of light barely cut through the dusty, cobwebby darkness as they scanned the entryway and stairs. Sheets covering the furniture made the house look like it had been decorated for a ghost party, and they were uninvited guests.

Hand in hand, they climbed the stairway. Every stair creaked or moaned. No wonder! The grand old house had been in the family for generations. It had been ransacked by soldiers near the end of the Civil War. Stories passed down through the family claimed that Confederate soldiers had stormed through the house, searching for something valuable. But that didn't make sense. It seemed more likely that Union soldiers had been responsible.

The girls explored room after room, sneezing as they pulled out drawers and poked under beds, disturbing years of dust. As they entered a bedroom, Laura hurried into the inky darkness. The floor creaked and cracked beneath her feet. Then, as if she'd been pulled from the room by a ghostly hand, Laura disappeared.

Meg screamed her sister's name as she rushed toward the spot where she'd vanished. She trained her flashlight on the floor. The pool of light disappeared into a huge, gaping hole. Dust motes sparkled in the beam of light that pooled on the floor below. In the middle of the floor, she saw her sister lying still, unmoving.

"Laura! Are you okay?" she yelled, forgetting in her fear that Laura couldn't hear her.

Trying not to panic, she raced down the staircase to the room into which she thought Laura had fallen. She wasn't there! Meg searched room after room. Laura wasn't in any of them! How could that be? She bolted back up the stairs to the room from which Laura had fallen and shined her light through the dark hole. Laura had managed to sit up, but she didn't seem to have her flashlight.

Meg chewed her lower lip. How could she find out where Laura was if they couldn't sign? She knelt down and set the flashlight on the floor so that it shined up on her, then signed, "I can't find you."

Then she picked up the light and shined it back on Laura. Laura signed, "I lost my flashlight. I can't find the door."

Meg put the light down again and signed, "Make some noise. Bang on something."

When she shined the light back on Laura, her sister nodded.

Meg hurried back downstairs, following the faint, hollow sound of her sister's thuds. The sound led her into a room filled with shelf after shelf of musty books. The noises echoed behind one of the bookshelves.

"A secret room!" Meg said. She tumbled books off the shelves until she found a small latch. When she lifted the latch, the whole wall moved inward. Meg leaned her shoulder against the wall; inch by inch, it squeaked open. She shined her flashlight across the floor. Laura grinned up at her.

Meg hurried to her side and helped her to her feet. "Let's get out of this place before anything else happens," she signed.

Laura pulled away, shaking her head. "Look," she signed.

Meg followed her pointing finger with the flashlight. A narrow cot and a washstand stood against one wall. A rickety wooden chest slouched beside it.

Limping a little, Laura moved toward the chest. Meg watched her sister open drawer after drawer. In the back of a bottom drawer, behind a stack of brittle, yellowed nightgowns, Laura found a plain wooden box. She placed it atop the chest and opened it slowly.

Expecting money or jewels or silverware, Meg shook her head and sighed when the box revealed nothing but crinkled, yellow papers.

She tugged at Laura's arm. "Let's get out of here," she signed. "This is a waste of time."

Laura shrugged her away. She rustled through the papers, unfolding them one by one. Meg peered over her shoulder as Laura ironed the final letter with her hand, then pointed to the signature at the bottom.

Laura signed out the letters of the signature one by one. "L-i-n-c-o-l-n."

"Abraham Lincoln!" Meg scanned the letter more closely. Her mouth dropped open. "Our ancestors were spies during the Civil War!" she signed.

Laura's eyes burned with excitement. She nodded.

Meg took a step back. She looked around the room once more. The small cot and washstand took on new significance. Had her ancestors hidden here as Confederate soldiers ransacked their house, looking for evidence of their guilt? Had they slipped away to the North? Or had the soldiers found and silenced them?

Meg glanced at the letter. Her ancestors had risked their lives for freedom and equality. Those were much greater treasures than money or jewels or silverware could ever be!

---

 **Comprehension Check**

1. Why does Laura think they will find a treasure in the boarded-up mansion?

2. Why do you think Meg believes that Union soldiers instead of Confederate soldiers may have ransacked the house?

3. Meg thinks that freedom and equality are much greater treasures than money or jewels or silverware. What is the greatest treasure that you have? Why?

4. The story of the treasure is passed down through Laura and Meg's family. What kinds of stories does your family pass down?

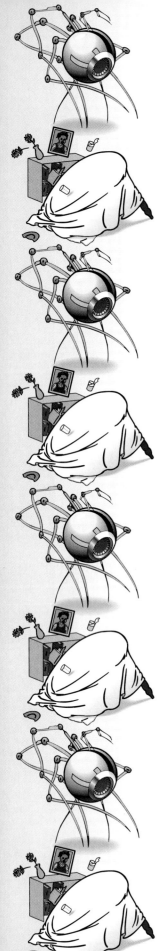

# Bugs to the Rescue!

*by Kim T. Griswell*

When the San Andreas Fault split open near Bodega Bay north of San Francisco, Paco Rios ducked under the heaviest piece of furniture he could find—the dining room table. His family's historic Marina district apartment building quivered like a sand castle dissolving in a wave. It had been 148 years since the great quake of 1906. He remembered his father saying that the further away in time you were from one big quake, the closer you were to the next one. This one felt big. Very, very big.

His mother was on the other side of the bay, working for Nanintech, a Silicon Valley lab that engineered nanobots, tiny microscopic machines that could do all kinds of miraculous things. Unfortunately, they couldn't prevent earthquakes.

"Paco!" His afterschool sitter, Mrs. Wilkins, rose from the couch and tried to walk across the room toward him, but the strength of the quake threw her to the floor.

With a series of cracks like a dozen strokes of lightning, the building seemed to drop from beneath them. Paco's stomach lurched upward. Something fell from the ceiling and crashed into the table. Two of its legs cracked like matchsticks, and the heavy table fell onto his leg. For a moment, a black haze oozed across his mind and he thought he would pass out.

When the building stopped shaking, the room was filled with dust. Paco could smell gas seeping from broken lines. It was a recipe for the kind of explosions and fire that had destroyed San Francisco in 1906. They had to get out of the building.

Then he saw Mrs. Wilkins. She lay on the floor just beyond the table. A knot the size of a golf ball rose on her forehead.

"Mrs. Wilkins?" He shoved at the table pinning his leg. A wave of pain and nausea washed over him. Somehow, he managed to get out from under the table and drag himself across the floor. The confetti of broken glass that glittered across the carpet bit into his palms.

"Mrs. Wilkins?" He shook her gently. When she didn't respond, he put his ear to her chest. Her heart beat erratically. He looked around the room, as if hoping the cracked walls and toppled shelves could somehow help her. Then he remembered his mother's bugs.

She always kept a few containers of micromechanical robots at home. She called them her little miracle workers. Though the microscopic nanobots were so small that thousands of them could sit on the head of a pin, they could be programmed to do incredible things. They'd been used to clean up an oil spill near Alaska by manipulating the atoms in the sludge to render it harmless. They could swim through a person's veins and repair damaged vessels or unclog arteries. With the right program, they could even repair broken bones.

Paco called them bugs. He didn't like them. Not at all. He imagined them crawling through the world like spider mites, invisible to the human eye but making mischief wherever they went.

"People are afraid of things they don't understand," his mom had said. "We've got the nanos totally under control. They can only do what we tell them to do. Take this container, for instance." She had pointed to something that looked like a Thermos® bottle on the desk in her home office. "These little guys can fix broken bones. No more casts. Isn't that cool?"

Paco looked at Mrs. Wilkins and thought about aftershocks and gas hissing from broken pipes. Even if he could get himself out of there, he couldn't get her out. Not with his leg broken.

"I'll be right back," he said, as if she could hear him.

As he crawled down the hall, the rafters moaned above his head, and dust from the ceiling tiles powdered his face. His hands felt cold, clammy. He wondered what would be worse: being crushed in the rubble or having medical nanobots, or medibots, madly rearranging the atoms of his body.

The nanobot container had rolled under his mother's desk. Paco screwed off the cap and peered inside. It looked empty, but his skin crawled at the thought of the billions of bugs just waiting to be released. He gritted his teeth and tipped the container over the place in his leg that hurt most. His skin began to tingle, then itch. He clenched his hands to keep from scratching. Then he waited. He had no idea how long it would take for the medibots to cure him.

As the minutes ticked by, he realized that the pain in his leg was fading to a warm glow. In a few more minutes, his leg felt normal. Gingerly, he got to his feet. His leg held. He hurried back down the hall.

The living room window had burst from its frame, leaving a gaping mouth filled with jagged glass teeth. He peered out, expecting to see a long drop to the ground. Incredibly, his apartment, which had been on the third floor, was now only one floor high. He hoisted Mrs. Wilkins onto his back and half carried, half dragged her toward the broken window. Somehow, he managed to lower her out the window onto a patch of grass. Then he hoisted himself over the windowsill and dropped down beside her.

Just as his feet touched the earth, another aftershock rocked the ground. Paco stumbled to his knees. As if the shock had jolted her awake, Mrs. Wilkins opened her eyes, blinking.

"Paco?" Her eyes tried to focus on him. "Are you okay?"

Paco nodded. "I'm fine. And you will be too. Thanks to some very helpful bugs!"

 ## Comprehension Check

1. How can you tell that this story takes place in the future?

2. Where does Paco's mother work?

3. Although Paco doesn't like the medibots, he decides to use them to heal his broken leg. Why does he make this decision?

4. Scientists are already developing nanotechnology similar to that described in this story. How would you feel about using the medibots to heal people?

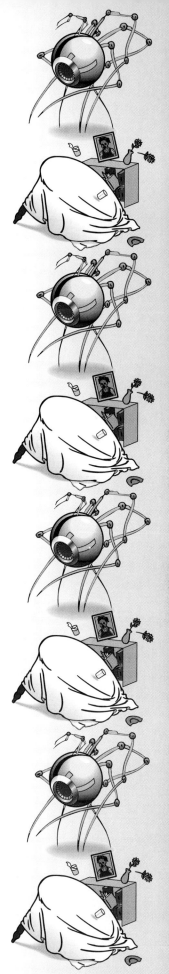

# The Great Dog Race

*by Tovah S. Yavin*

Buddy zigzagged through the tall grass like a perpetual motion machine that could not be stopped.

"Come on, Buddy! You can find it!" Ben yelled.

Buddy sniffed this way, then that way, scrutinizing one side of the field and then the other side of the field. Ben wasn't worried; Buddy would find the ball. He was a first-class hound dog.

Robo used a different method. He didn't zig or zag or sniff. He pointed his triangular ears toward one side of the field. His mouth sent out beeping sounds. The computer in his nose added, subtracted, multiplied, and did other arithmetic things that Ben had never even heard of. Then he would roll forward a short distance, twist his ears a different way, and start all over again.

"To your right, Buddy!" Ben screamed. "Go to your right!"

"Hush," Roy said. "Your screaming will confuse Robo's beeps."

"You mean the new, wonderful, D500-model hound dog gets confused by a little noise? Too bad. You gotta expect a little noise during a race."

And that's what this was: the great dog race. Buddy, a real dog, was pitted against Robo, the newest, greatest robotic dog you could buy. Ben's dad wouldn't buy him a robot dog. He didn't believe in all these newfangled machines, but that was okay. Ben preferred Buddy, the best hound dog in the world.

"Come on, Buddy! You're heading the wrong way!" Ben screamed as loudly as he could. If crowd noise confused Robo, then Ben was going to make all the noise he could. Especially since the rest of the crowd, Ben's sister and Roy's sister, was just sitting on a bench, quietly watching the race.

"Ruby! Make some noise!" Ben yelled to his little sister. Ruby rolled her eyes toward the sky and put her hands over her ears. Great, Ben thought. Why couldn't he have a sister who would help him out when he needed it?

So far the contest was one to one. Ben and Roy had agreed on a three-part contest to decide which dog was best. Robo won the jumping contest right away. When Roy pushed a button on his remote control, the spring in Robo's belly shot out and launched him like a rocket. Buddy got so nervous he refused to jump at all.

Then Buddy won the eating part of the contest: who coud eat the most food the fastest. Robo's stomach slot got all stuffed up. That left the ball chase. The winner of this event would be declared the best dog in the neighborhood.

Robo's beeping mouth, twisty ears, and intelligent nose worked very well. He located his ball while Buddy was still sniffing through the tall grass.

"Get the ball, Buddy! Come on, boy!" Ben pleaded.

This time when Roy pushed a button on his remote control, nothing happened.

"Hey! What's going on? Robo's jaw is stuck!"

Just then Buddy found his ball and meandered back toward his master, drool dripping from his jaws.

"Robo's broken," Roy whined as he angrily pushed the button on his remote control. "His jaw won't move."

"Hurry, Buddy!" Ben yelled. "Let's terminate this mechanical pooch!"

Then Roy jabbed a different button, transmitting a different signal, and suddenly Robo's head tilted backward. His jaw was still stuck open, but with his head tilted back, the ball was nestled safely in his mouth. Next, Roy made Robo's leg wheels start spinning.

"Run, Buddy!"

As his wheels spun faster, Robo headed across the field with a vengeance.

"Go, Buddy!"

Robo accelerated past Buddy.

"Hurry, Buddy!"

Buddy hurried as fast as he could. Robo's wheels spun so fast, Ben expected them to start smoking any minute. Then Robo stopped suddenly and did a triple-loop somersault through the air, landing squarely on his back. The ball rolled out of Robo's mouth and across the grass.

"That's not fair!" Roy stamped his foot. "Robo hit a rock!"

"Hah!" Ben cheered. "Buddy can just jump over rocks."

Buddy romped across the finish line, his long ears waving, his tongue dribbling, his tail wagging. The great Robo, model D500, had lost to a real first-class hound dog. Just as Ben bent down to give Buddy a big hug, thunder rumbled across the field. Then Ben felt a drop of rain, followed by a second and a third.

Ben's sister and Roy's robot sister scurried over. Ben's sister took Buddy's leash for the walk home. Roy pushed a button on his remote, making his sister's two mechanical arms lift up while he attached a large, waterproof cloth to her hands. Roy stepped onto the little platform attached to her legs, then set her speed dial and direction finder for home. Ben watched her wheels spin down the street, with Roy and Robo riding comfy and dry.

Buddy gave his long ears a shake, sending out a few raindrops, as Ben and his sister led Buddy home. Ben decided he would never want a robot dog, but a robot sister didn't sound bad at all!

 ## Comprehension Check

1. What is unusual about the race in this story?

2. Although this race is literally just a race between Buddy and Robo, what does this race seek to prove about real dogs and robot dogs?

3. Why does Buddy win the race?

4. Why do you think Ben feels that a robot sister wouldn't be bad at all?

# The Carousel

*by Kim T. Griswell*

The eerie music coming from the old carousel drew Jamil toward the darkest end of the street. Everything else on this side of town was dying, but the carousel just kept running. Garish lights outlined every surface, making the whole thing glow. The teenager selling tickets wore an apron around his waist with two big pockets: one for tickets, the other for money. He must be a pretty brave dude, Jamil thought, to be down here all alone with money in his pockets.

The neighborhood seemed to get scarier every day, and the scariest thing was thinking he'd never get out. Jamil lived with his Aunt Eustice in an apartment building made of blue cement blocks. Hopelessness and fear hung over the place like a cold fog. His aunt tried to encourage him by saying things like, "Just because you were born on the south side, doesn't mean you have to stay here. The only ones who don't make it out are those too scared to try."

The carousel guy waved him over. "How about a ride?"

Jamil shook his head. "No way, man. I'm too old for that thing."

From far away, the guy's eyes seemed perfectly normal. But up close, Jamil could see that he had one blue eye and one eye that was white and misty, shimmering like an opal. To keep from staring, he read the nametag pinned to the teen's faded football jersey. "Ezekial." What kind of old-timey name was that?

Ezekial must have noticed the look on his face because he grinned.

"Most folks call me Zeke," he said.

"What's up, Zeke?" Jamil nodded.

"Not much these days," Zeke admitted. "But if you'd like to take a ride, it's on the house." He winked his blue eye and stared at Jamil with the misty one. Jamil shivered. His aunt always said "Cat walked over your grave" when something made him feel this creepy.

"You know," Zeke said, "this is no ordinary carousel."

"Is that so?" Jamil slumped back on his heels.

Zeke nodded. "Hang on a minute. Got to prime the works before your ride."

He hopped up onto the platform before Jamil could remind him that he wasn't about to ride any carousel. Once he reached the mirrored center, Zeke stepped down and grabbed a knob Jamil couldn't see. One of the mirrored panels swung wide for a second as Zeke ducked inside.

Jamil expected to see an electric panel and a bunch of gears at the center of the carousel. Instead, the door opened into seething blackness, punctuated by a swirling mass of stars so bright he had to close his eyes to keep them from burning. Jamil felt like the concrete had melted beneath his feet. His knees wobbled. When he opened his eyes, the door was closed. All he could see was his paled face in the mirror.

Zeke reappeared at his side so suddenly that Jamil jumped. Then he slouched back again and stuffed his hands in the deep pockets of his baggy jeans so Zeke couldn't see them shaking.

"You ready?" Zeke asked.

What was he to do, say no, I'm too scared to ride your carousel? Jamil nodded.

"Then hop aboard."

Jamil grabbed the pole holding up the closest animal—a black stallion showing all its teeth in a maniacal whinny.

Zeke held up a hand. "Choose carefully," he said. "Only one of these will take you where you need to go. The others will just take you around and around in circles."

Jamil backed away from the black horse and walked slowly around the platform.

He bypassed a bunny with three-foot-long ears. He ducked around a cat clutching a turquoise fish in its mouth. Then he came face-to-face with a huge gray boar with painted bristles. Its fat red tongue thrust out of its mouth between huge white tusks. It dared him to get on with the same look his aunt gave him when she dared him to stay in school.

Jamil put his face right up to the boar's, looked him eye to eye. "Time to ride," he said. He tucked the toe of his high-top into the stirrup, grabbed the pole, and swung up.

Zeke waved as he pushed a red button on the panel beside the ticket stand. Jamil gripped the pole as the carousel started to turn slowly. As he came around the second time, Jamil noticed that Zeke was starting to blur. The third time around, Zeke looked like those streaks of light in movies that have been speeded up. Jamil's stomach felt like it wanted to turn itself inside out.

The boar lurched up and down. Up and down. The smooth, painted skin beneath his hands began to feel coarse, like it was covered with bristles. Jamil jerked his hands away. The boar's head reared back. Jamil tumbled off. He didn't land on the platform, but in coarse underbrush. Thorns pierced his hands and scratched his face as he fought his way to his feet. Something pawed and snuffled on the other side.

"Zeke?" he whispered. His voice quivered, but he took a deep breath and parted the bushes.

Once again, he was eye to eye with the boar, but this time, the boar was alive. It stood three feet tall and looked like it weighed about 400 pounds. Thick tusks sprouted from its powerful jaws. Its beady black eyes looked very, very angry.

Surrounded by thorn bushes, Jamil could hardly move. The only way out was forward, right onto the path where the boar was kicking up dust and preparing to charge.

"Now what, Aunt Eustice? You got any homegrown wisdom for something like this?" Jamil said aloud.

The boar snorted and tossed back its head.

Then Jamil remembered what his aunt said about sticky situations. "When you get yourself into a sticky situation, the only way out is to move forward."

Jamil took a deep breath. If he could get free of the bushes, he could run. He counted to ten, then flung himself out of the bushes. His feet felt like they would catch fire, but no matter how fast he ran, the boar stayed right behind him, its tusks inches behind him. Pretty soon, he realized he kept passing the same things. The same thorn bushes. The same spindly trees. He was running in circles.

"Now what?" he silently asked Aunt Eustice. The answer came in that molasses-thick voice she used when she'd repeated something one time too many. "Jamil, you will never get ahead in life unless you learn to face your fears."

"Easy for her to say," he puffed. She didn't have a 400-pound boar on her heels. He was beginning to tire. He could feel the boar's hot breath through his shirt. Maybe just once he should take his aunt's advice: stop running and face his fears. He counted down from ten, slowing with each number. Strangely, the boar stayed one step behind. When he reached zero, he stopped, turned, and looked the boar right in the eye.

It stopped. Drool dripped from its tusks, but it didn't move. In fact, it looked frozen, like a statue. Its hide had this weird painted gloss to it. Jamil reached out a shaking hand, felt the cool, smooth surface of a carousel animal. Waves started rolling in his stomach again. His head felt like a helium balloon that some kid had let go.

He was back on the carousel. His hands clutched the pole above the boar's head

so hard his knuckles turned white. The ride slowed, then stopped. Jamil wobbled off.

"Was it eventful?" Zeke's eye shimmered.

Jamil wiped sweat from his forehead. "Eventful?" He caught his breath and turned on Zeke. "Man, I could have died on that thing! I thought I'd never get out of there!"

Zeke held up his hands. "There's only one way out," he said. "Out of there," he pointed at the carousel, "or out of here." A sweep of his hands took in the decaying street, the neighborhood surrounding it. "And you found it."

"Face your fears?" Jamil asked.

Zeke nodded. "Now that you've done it once, you can do it again." He winked that one blue eye, but this time Jamil saw hope in the shimmering opal that kept staring at him.

"Yeah," he said. "I guess I can."

 ## Comprehension Check

**1.** What is happening in Jamil's neighborhood?

**2.** Why do you think Jamil's aunt gives him the kind of advice she does?

**3.** What does Zeke mean when he says, "Only one of these will take you where you need to go"?

**4.** Do you think Jamil's carousel ride might change his life? If so, how? If not, why not?

# Dinosaur Discoveries

*by Pamela F. Service*

"The dinosaurs didn't become extinct," Travis's grandfather said while fixing their peanut butter sandwiches. "They migrated."

Travis liked his grandfather and was glad his parents were having him stay with Gramps while they were in Georgia researching their family tree. But Gramps didn't seem to quite have all of his senses. He wondered if his parents recognized this. Better to humor him than to argue.

"Migrated? Where'd they go?" Travis asked.

"Out there somewhere." Gramps gestured to the ceiling with his peanut-buttery knife. "They knew an asteroid was going to hit Earth and would wipe out most of the life here. They were quite good astronomers. So they left."

"Right," Travis said, accepting his sandwich. "In spaceships?"

Gramps nodded, taking a bite of his own sandwich.

Travis had to argue a little. "But how come we haven't found their telescopes or spaceships or anything? I mean, you worked for years as a paleontologist, and all you ever told me about finding were bones."

"Well, of course. Bones become fossilized. But a telescope wouldn't fossilize. It'd just rust. Scientists digging around millions of years later would never find it."

Travis wondered if Gramps had retired from the university's paleontology department or if he'd really been fired for having such crazy ideas.

"But dinosaurs had really small brains, didn't they? How could they build spaceships?" wondered Travis.

"Size isn't everything. Their brains evolved differently. After all, dinosaurs were on Earth far longer than we humans. They had time to evolve quite a bit of intelligence," explained Gramps.

"Okay, but if they didn't leave any record of their being so smart and building machines, how come you know about it?"

"They've told me."

Travis choked on his sandwich, and Gramps hastily added, "Well, not the ones who migrated, of course. Their descendants. They leave their planet sometimes and come back here to do genealogy research. Looking for their roots, like your folks are doing now in Georgia. Sometimes they'd come by the department when I was working there, and I'd help them out. Made some close friends that way."

"So you'd show them the fossils?" Travis asked.

"Yes, they were quite touched by them, sometimes said prayers over them and got kind of weepy. Then I'd usually tell them places they could go to see fossils actually in the ground. Wyoming and Mongolia and such," said Gramps.

Travis didn't know if he should play along with this fantasy any longer, but then Gramps changed the subject. "Well, what shall we have for dinner tonight? Spaghetti or barbecued chicken?"

"Er, chicken, I guess."

"My choice too, but I've got to go to the store and get some more briquettes for the grill." He stood up from the kitchen table and plucked his jacket off a peg.

At the door, Gramps turned. "I won't be gone long, but in case I'm delayed I'd better tell you that I've been baby-sitting for some friends. If they come for their little one while I'm away, just hand him over and give them my best."

He reached into a cupboard beside the stove, handed Travis a blanket-wrapped bundle, and opened the door. "Keep him warm."

Travis unwrapped the bundle once Gramps was gone. A rock. A smooth, rounded

rock. Okay, now it seemed that his grandfather was a little crazy. He wondered if he should call his parents. No, Gramps seemed harmlessly crazy.

Walking into the den, Travis switched on the TV to take his mind off everything. He tucked the blanketed rock beside him so Gramps could see what a good baby-sitter he was.

Partway through a nature show, the doorbell rang. Travis opened the door to see a tall couple in floppy hats that nearly covered their faces and long coats that reached the ground. "My grandfather's not in," he said.

"Ah! His grandson! The professor's talked so much about you. Sorry we can't stay until his return, but we must be off to Mongolia, you know. We've just come for Junior."

"Junior?" Travis asked blankly.

"Well, Junior-to-be." The woman giggled. "Ah, there he is," she added, pointing to the wrapped rock on the couch.

Numbly, Travis retrieved the bundle and handed it over. The hands he placed it in were very scaly, and the smiles that thanked him had very pointy teeth.

When Travis returned to the couch, he switched off the TV. He had some major rethinking to do about everything he thought he knew about dinosaurs and about his grandfather.

 ## Comprehension Check

1. Why does Travis think Gramps is crazy?

2. Gramps refers to an asteroid when he talks about the dinosaurs leaving the earth. What do you think he is talking about?

3. Travis thinks his grandfather has left him in charge of a rock wrapped in a blanket. What has he really left him?

4. What do you think Earth would be like if dinosaurs had evolved along with humans?

# All That Glitters

*by Kim T. Griswell*

Gideon kept the box in the top drawer of his bedside table. It was plain, as boxes go, nothing ornate. In fact, it looked more like a fat black cube than a box. Gideon alone knew that the box would open only when someone uttered the right phrase. Gold-flecked light would spill from within to bathe anything near it with the toasty feeling of curling up in front of a fireplace. It was Gideon's most treasured possession, more important to him than his in-line skates or his telescope, or even his computer. His mother had given it to him when he was five years old.

"I want you to remember what's really important. All that glitters is not gold. Hugs." She'd hugged him close. "Time together. Love and goodness. Those things can't be bought. Keep this box safe," she'd whispered, "and I'll always be near."

She'd died not long after. Cancer had eaten away the healthy cells in her body, his father said, but it couldn't touch the memories Gideon kept in his heart.

Gideon never shared the box with anyone. Then Lucia moved into the neighborhood and sucked all of Gideon's friends into the blinding whirl of her life.

Lucia had everything. Her father was a dotcom gazillionaire. Their house on the hill looked like a castle, complete with moat—a recycling river that Lucia and her friends floated along in overinflated inner tubes. A blue and yellow banner fluttered in the breeze above the castle, emblazoned with the trademark symbol of her father's company: a lightning bolt zapping a book.

"It means," Lucia said when Gideon asked, "that thanks to my dad's company, everything you've ever wanted to know can be found at the speed of lightning."

Gideon shrugged. "I've tried using your dad's search engine. Those lightning-fast three-line answers don't really answer much of anything. I might as well ask a question of a Magic Eight Ball®."

Lucia's face turned red. Her fingers clenched. "What do you know?" she asked. "Investors from all over the world have poured money into my dad's company." Her face, which had looked as happy as peppermint ice cream suddenly turned to sour spinach. "He works all day and all night and he's never home and it's worth every sacrifice he's made." Her eyes had a wet sparkle and he wondered if the fairy-tale castle on the hill was as happy as it looked.

After that, Lucia stopped inviting Gideon to the castle. His friends drifted away one by one. For the first time since his mom died, he felt totally alone.

The invitation to Lucia's birthday party nearly knocked him off his feet when he pulled it out of the mailbox. Gideon racked his brain for a gift suitable for a girl who had everything. Then he remembered the box. He couldn't give her that, of course, but what if he gave her just one glimpse of what it held? Her father's money had bought her plenty of things, but it hadn't taken the sour-spinach look off her face. His box could do that.

At her party, Gideon took Lucia aside while the other kids were stuffing their faces with slices of blackberry truffle cake.

"My mom made me invite you," she said before he could even get the box from his pack.

The heat rising up the back of his neck wasn't from the press of people in the room.

"And I'm glad you didn't waste your money buying me a present. As you can see, I've got everything I could ever want already."

Gideon clutched the box in his hands. This was stupid. The box probably wouldn't even work for someone like Lucia. Could the golden warmth it emanated melt those ice cube eyes?

"My present's in here," he said at last.

"In there? Looks like that dumb eight ball you think you can find answers in." She sighed. "Boring."

Gideon cradled the box in his hands. "It's not boring. Look." He bent over the box and whispered, "All that glitters is not gold."

The box whooshed open and gold-flecked light spilled onto his hands, then wafted into the air like smoke. The glittery air settled over Lucia and she drew in a sharp breath.

"What, what is it?" Lucia stammered.

Gideon grinned. "My mom gave it to me," he said.

Lucia shook her head. She blinked back tears. "It—it's horrible. Why did you bring that thing here? It's making me sad, sad, sad!"

"Sad?" Gideon asked, wrinkling his nose. "How could it make you sad?"

"Because," she sniffed, "it's like Christmas and baking cookies with your mom and your dad reading you a bedtime story all wrapped up in one!"

"What's sad about that?" he asked.

"What's sad is that those things are history. No one does them anymore. Everyone just rushes from here to there and back again," Lucia explained.

"At the speed of lightning?"

She nodded, blinking back tears. "Yes."

"So what's wrong with slowing down?" he asked.

"My dad says if you slow down, you get left behind," answered Lucia.

Gideon shook his head. "You don't get left behind. You catch up with what's important."

It was Lucia's turn to look bewildered.

"All that glitters is not gold," he said.

"What's that supposed to mean, anyway?"

"It means that there are some pretty wonderful things that have nothing to do with money."

Lucia wiped tears from her face with the back of her hand. "Tell that to my dad," she said.

Suddenly, Gideon knew what to do. His memories of his mother were tucked in his heart. He didn't need the box to keep them there. He handed it to Lucia.

"Maybe this will help him remember," he said.

---

 # Comprehension Check

**1.** Why is the box so special to Gideon?

**2.** What do you think the phrase "all that glitters is not gold" means?

**3.** Lucia has everything money can buy. Do you think she's happy? Why or why not?

**4.** What is the most special thing anyone has ever given you? What makes it special?

# The Rock Collectors

*by Pamela F. Service*

Scott felt the rocks and the cold right through his sleeping bag. He didn't care; his parents were finally letting him sleep outside the tent. In midwestern campgrounds, the tent at least kept out mosquitoes. Now that they'd reached the western desert, mosquitoes were scarce, but the tent was still crowded, smelly, and filled with his dad's snores.

Out here, the cold, silent air smelled of sage. Scrunching up in the sleeping bag till only his face was exposed, Scott gazed at the stars. There were millions of stars, billions. He never saw this many in the city. These didn't twinkle; they glinted like chips of ice.

There were supposed to be meteors tonight. He'd already seen three. Another! He wanted to stay awake and count them. Silently, another cut across the Big Dipper. A breeze rattled the sagebrush, and coyotes yapped in the distance.

When Scott looked again at the sky, he realized he'd fallen asleep. The constellations had shifted, and a glow already shone in the east. Annoyed that he'd missed most of the meteors, he rolled to look at the dawn. Odd. The glow wasn't rosy; it was blue, artificial, and it wasn't coming from the horizon but from down the arroyo below their camp.

Was someone else camped down there? No, the light appeared too cold for a campfire. Not headlights either, he decided. Wriggling out of his sleeping bag, he slipped on cold boots and stood up, but he couldn't see far enough into the arroyo.

Ignoring the cold, he trudged to where the rocky ground sloped down to the dry riverbed. The luminous blue light shone stronger, but through the sagebrush he couldn't see its source. Its light was enough for him to creep down a little gully. At the bottom, he peered over a boulder. Astonished, he dropped down.

Had he really seen what he thought? Cautiously he stuck his head up again. There was a vehicle, but it wasn't a car. It was the size of a house, a big house. Shaped like an upside-down bowl, it glowed blue. Scott squinted against the eerie light. Blue figures moved in and out of a doorway in the bowl's side.

A spaceship, he realized with cold, sickening certainty. What should he do? Run to the tent and wake his parents? No. His mom might get hysterical; his dad would think he was a lunatic. And if they didn't think he was crazy—if they actually believed him—that might even be worse! His dad had the cell phone. He'd call the police or the army, maybe even the Pentagon. They'd show up with guns and helicopters and drive the spaceship away. Scott wanted to discover what the blue figures were doing, not scare them into the next galaxy.

His eyes finally adjusted to the light. Now he could see that the figures were carrying things into the ship, things that looked like rocks. They were picking up rocks from the riverbed and carrying them inside. Why? Were they intergalactic rock collectors? Did they use rocks for fuel? Maybe they ate rocks. It didn't matter. There were plenty of rocks around. Their taking a few rocks was no reason to call the army.

Hearing a scraping sound behind him, Scott spun around. A startled blue alien stood a few feet away. It was short. A kid? Its eyes were wide, and it opened its thin mouth, then closed it again. They looked silently at each other. Scott carefully crouched down and picked up a smooth gray rock. Cautiously, he offered it to the alien.

The blue mouth didn't smile, but the skin around the eyes crinkled. An arm with two elbows reached out. Eight blue fingers wrapped around the rock, touching Scott. They felt warm.

Scott watched the short figure walk back to the others. Would it tell? It didn't seem to. The aliens gathered rocks a while longer, then filed into the glowing bowl. Almost the last one in, the short one glanced back toward Scott's boulder, then turned and proceeded inside.

Scott watched the ship ascend and disappear into the real dawn, a tiny star in a rosy sky. Then he descended into the arroyo. There was no sign that anything had been there, not even an indentation pressed into the sand. Then he noticed something glinting on a large, flat rock. Exhilarated, he hurried over. It was another rock, a blue one. Scott picked it up. It felt warm in his hand and seemed to be illuminated from inside by shifting waves of blue light. Its shimmering surface looked like pictures of the ocean as seen from space.

"Well, Scott, you're up exploring early," his dad called from the top of the arroyo. "Did you enjoy sleeping out?"

"Yeah," Scott called back, slipping the rock into his pocket. "The desert's an interesting place at night."

## Comprehension Check

1. Why is Scott sleeping outside the tent?

2. Where is his family camping?

3. Why do you think Scott and the small blue alien keep the fact that they've seen each other to themselves?

4. What would you do if you met an alien?

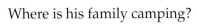

# The Egghead Edge

*by Kim T. Griswell*

Xijohn shaded his eyes as he stared up at the star. Waves of fire seemed to jet from Alpha Centauri. Even inside the air-conditioned dome, he could feel Centauri's rays burning his exposed skin. Though it seemed like centuries ago, it had only been 40 years since the Hubble Space Telescope pinpointed Exodus orbiting Alpha Centauri, the brilliant star 4.35 light-years from Earth's familiar sun. Twenty more years passed before NASA's scientists perfected interstellar travel. Distances that once would have taken many human lifetimes could now be traveled in the blink of an eye.

"Hey, Xi! You gonna play or stargaze?" called a voice from the other end of the smaquet court.

Xijohn waved to his team's captain, Asianna. "Okay, okay! I'll be there in a sec."

Smaquet was a cross between soccer and racquetball. The balls were formed from a superspringy material made from the sap of trees found in the fiery tropics. The four players on the offensive team bounced a two-inch ball down the court on elbows, knees, or heads. They scored by using a racket to smash the ball past the other team's defense into the hot pink electronic buzzer set in the wall behind the goal line. The players wore antigravity devices that allowed them to hover above the floor and travel by pushing off the floor and padded walls.

Because the atmospheric pressure on Exodus was one and a half times that of Earth's, the old Earth games had to be adapted. The first astronauts who landed had tried a game of touch football, but the players began to drop like flies after half a quarter. The air was just too hot and heavy.

Xijohn was a smasher for the Engineers. It was his job to hit the ball into the buzzer once his teammates got it to him. They were in the final game of a series that had left them tied two to two with their rivals, the Pilots. The score was 53 to 52, in the Engineers' favor. If they won, it would be the first time in the team's history.

Xijohn wanted to win this game more than he'd ever wanted anything. He'd had all he could take of the Pilots' teasing.

"You egghead Engineers can't do anything without a schematic!" the Pilots' captain, Raythan, jeered.

Xijohn hefted his new graphite racket from hand to hand, blowing on his palms to dry the sweat. He'd show Raythan that he didn't need a diagram to play the game. He adjusted his eye protectors and waved at Asianna.

"Set!" he called, as he turned off his antigravity device and planted his feet a few inches in front of the Pilots' goal line. Smashers always anchored to the ground before trying to score.

As Asianna swooshed toward him, Raythan turned off his antigravity device and landed like a marble statue in front of her. Flying nearly weightlessly, Asianna slammed into him with such force that she hurtled backward into the wall.

"Foul!" Xijohn shouted.

The referee blew a whistle in agreement. Only smashers were allowed to turn off antigravity devices, and then only when they were set to score.

Asianna wobbled to her feet, shook her head, and waved a hand to the ref.

"Ball to the Engineers at Pilot goal line!" he shouted.

Raythan's foul gave Xijohn one free shot at the Pilots' goal. Xijohn focused on the target, tossed the ball into the air, cocked his elbow, and slammed the ball into the buzzer. He didn't have time to celebrate their two-point lead. The ball bounced off the wall and ricocheted down the court. The Pilots' smasher drove it into their buzzer for three points. The crowd rose to its feet and cheers bounced off the dome's rounded walls.

"Score Pilots!" announced the computer.

Xijohn looked up at the scoreboard. The Pilots were now ahead by one point with only 20 seconds to go. Xijohn's stomach lurched. Maybe Raythan was right. He'd spent a lot of time memorizing plays, but what good did that do him on the court? Could a bunch of egghead Engineers ever beat the famous Pilots?

Asianna had just smacked the ball to one of their best long-hitters. She motioned Xijohn to the far right. Then she gave him a play signal he'd couldn't remember seeing before. He wracked his brain, trying to pull up the picture of the play as he flipped on his antigravity device and swooped across the court. Shaking his head, he switched off the antigravity device, planted his feet, and called, "Set!"

Raythan darted down the court and began to zip back and forth in front of Xijohn. The ball was coming in high. Too high. Xijohn would never be able to reach it from the ground. What was Asianna thinking?

Just before the ball reached him, he remembered the play. He flipped on his antigravity device and sprang into the air.

Raythan snickered, "That's right, Engineer. Might as well give up. This game is over."

Xijohn ignored him as he cocked back his arm and smashed the ball toward the buzzer.

"Hey! That's not legal!" Raythan yelled.

"Score Engineers!" the computer announced just as the clock ran out.

Raythan's mouth dropped open. Since the computer had every play entered into its data banks, it could not award a point scored on an illegal play. The Engineers had won.

Xijohn flipped off his antigravity device and sank to the ground.

"I've never seen a smasher hit from off the ground," Raythan said. "How'd you know it was legal?"

Xijohn grinned. "Must have been those schematics," he said.

 **Comprehension Check**

1. Where does this story take place?

2. What are some of the rules of smaquet?

3. Do you think the schematics help Xijohn win the game? Why or why not?

4. Even on Earth, sports differ from place to place. What sports played in other countries can you think of that are different than those played in your country?

# Showboat

*by Kim T. Griswell*

Mari's stallion, Sybaris, could do two things really well—run and dance. She had discovered his most unusual talent when he was just a colt. While mucking out his stall, she'd been listening to a CD featuring jazz great Louis Armstrong. Sybaris had lifted his head from his feed bag as if listening. In a few minutes, he began to prance from side to side, in time to the music.

Though her father thought training a thoroughbred racehorse to dance distracted him from his real work, Mari disagreed.

"Think of it as recreation. Sybaris trains hard. He deserves some fun."

"Okay," her father agreed at last. "But just around here. If anyone sees that horse dancing, I'll be laughed off the racetrack."

Each evening Mari played Louis Armstrong tunes while the mahogany red thoroughbred bopped his muscular haunches to the beat.

A few evenings before the County Fair Race, Jason Reivers from the neighboring horse farm stumbled into her session with Sybaris. He pointed a finger at the stallion and snickered.

"What on earth is that horse doing?" he asked.

Mari quickly turned off the CD player and settled Sybaris with a pat on the neck. "Nothing," she said.

Jason shook his head. "My dad always said Creekmore Farms had some interesting training methods, but this one takes the cake!"

Jason's teasing felt like a burr beneath a saddle blanket, but Mari shrugged nonchalantly, as if she didn't care.

"Don't you have somewhere to go?" she asked, reaching down for a currycomb.

When Jason left, all Mari could think about was the trouble she'd be in if he spread the news about Sybaris. They'd be the laughingstock of the racetrack.

By Saturday, she'd chewed her nails to the quick worrying, but so far not a peep had been said about Creekmore Farms's dancing horse. Maybe Jason wasn't as big a pest as she thought.

When they arrived at the fairgrounds, Mari gave Sybaris a last hug for luck, then left him with her father and his jockey. She hurried out to the track, keeping an eye open for Jason. She spotted him near the fence. He was carrying a boom box in one hand and a supersize soda in the other. She watched until he'd seated himself near the first turn; then she went in the opposite direction. Maybe he'd forgotten the whole thing.

Pretty soon, the horses were at the starting line. With a shot that jolted Mari to her feet, they were off. Sybaris jumped out a full head in front of the others. Jason's horse, Blue Streak, stayed a few strides back. By the time they neared the first turn, Sybaris was three lengths ahead of the field. Excitement bubbled in Mari's stomach like a fizzy soda; if he kept up this pace, Sybaris was sure to win.

Then, just as he entered the turn, he hesitated, his footing becoming uncertain. As the horse lost his momentum, Mari raised her binoculars. The jockey seemed to be fighting with the reins as Sybaris broke his stride and began to bump his hips back and forth.

A wave of laughter rolled through the crowd.

"Oh, no!" Mari whispered.

Blue Streak blurred past the jittery Sybaris. As the jockey urged the horse forward, the rest of the field caught up and parted around them like water around a boulder. Once the jockey managed to wrestle Sybaris out of the turn, the horse seemed to remember how to run. He leapt forward, his ears and head low as his hooves tossed up dirt clods.

"Yes!" Mari smacked a fist into her palm. "Go, boy!" she yelled.

The jockey tucked in and pushed Sybaris back to the front of the field, but when they reached the third turn, he began to hesitate again.

Lifting her binoculars, Mari aimed them toward the stands. Most of the crowd were on their feet, but she spotted Jason crouched near the fence, fiddling with a knob on his boom box.

Something strange is going on over there, Mari decided. She left her seat and hurried around the track, trying to keep an eye on both Jason and Sybaris. The boy had a great big grin on his face, while the horse looked wide-eyed, uncertain. As she got closer, she began to hear a familiar honey-sweet beat: Louis Armstrong belting out "What a Wonderful World."

Jason was playing jazz on his boom box. No wonder the jockey had to fight so hard to move Sybaris out of the turn!

Blue Streak broke for the stretch. If the horses reached the turn again before she got to Jason, the race would be over. Mari bumped and pushed her way through the crowd. Just as the horses reached the turn, Louis Armstrong started to sing. Mari surged forward and jabbed the off button.

"Hey!" Jason jerked the boom box away. "What do you think you're doing?"

Mari glared. "I should be asking you that!" she said.

Jason shrugged. "That horse of yours is nothing but a showboat. He's not a race-horse. Did you see him out there shimmying to the beat? What a joke!"

Mari clenched her fists and turned to watch the end of the race. Come on, Sybaris, she urged. You're not a joke. You're multitalented. You can dance and you can run. Now run!

Sybaris's flying feet ate up the turf as the front-runners thundered down the home-stretch. Just as they reached the wire, he pulled alongside Blue Streak, stretched out his long, graceful neck, and nosed ahead.

Mari jumped up and down, then turned to Jason.

"Guess you were right," she said.

"About what?" He blinked.

"About my horse being a showboat. He really showed you!"

---

 ## Comprehension Check

**1.** How does Mari first discover her horse's talent for dancing?

**2.** Why doesn't Mari's father want anyone to know that Sybaris can dance?

**3.** What kind of person do you think Jason Reivers is? Why?

**4.** If you were Mari, what would you do about Jason's raceside trick?

# The Perfect Pet

*by Danielle S. Hammelef*

Ever since David could remember, he'd wanted a pet. His parents always said, "You're too young," and gave him stuffed animals instead. He had enough stuffed tigers, elephants, dogs, monkeys, and giraffes to open a zoo.

As he grew older, they said pets were too messy or they didn't have enough room for a pet in their small apartment or they couldn't afford to feed a pet. One day, after a marathon session of begging, his dad presented him with a small cardboard box with holes punched in the top. "Here you go, David. Your very own pet!"

At last! Pet possibilities crawled, swam, slithered, crept, hopped, purred, and wriggled through his head.

Was it a puppy or a kitten? No, the box was too small.

A hamster? A mouse? A rat? No, the thought of rodents made his mom shiver. So it probably wasn't a guinea pig either.

Tarantula! No, it couldn't be. He could still hear his dad yell, "Forget it!"

Monkey? No, Mom said they were too exotic. He'd looked up *exotic.* It meant "different or unusual." David decided his grandparents were exotic.

His smile felt much too big for his face as he snatched the box from his dad's hands. He held the box to his ear. "I don't hear anything," he said, his smile fading. "I can't feel it moving." He tried to peek through the tiny airholes, but couldn't see a thing.

"I think it's sleeping, maybe even hibernating." His dad grinned.

A turtle! David pried open the lid as gently as he could, resisting his instinct to rip it off and meet his new friend. What he saw in the box melted his rising hopes faster than an open flame under ice cream: two plastic eyes glued to an ordinary, gray, fist-sized rock.

He tried to laugh it off, to keep his disappointment from showing, but there must have been something in his face that exposed his real feelings.

"Come on, buddy," his dad encouraged. "You can keep it on your nightstand. You'll never have to feed it or walk it."

"Or play with it," David mumbled, thunking the rock back into the box and shutting the lid.

He'd had enough. There had to be a pet that his parents would let him have. The next day, David headed to the pet store to find the perfect pet. He described the kind of pet he wanted to the girl behind the counter.

"It has to be housebroken. It must be friendly. It has to live longer than a hamster, but not as long as a guinea pig. It can't have beady eyes or carry diseases. It can't be messy or dangerous. And it can't be exotic."

The girl frowned. "Sorry, but we don't have anything like that," she said. "You need to go to the toy store."

David frowned. "They have pets at the toy store?"

"Yeah, stuffed pets!" The girl laughed. "That's the only kind of pet that fits your description."

David's shoulders sagged; he'd never have a pet. He spun from the counter and smacked right into Mrs. Palmer, his neighbor from across the hall.

"Are you looking for a pet, too?" she asked.

David shook his head. "I can't find one that my parents will let me have."

Mrs. Palmer's eyes looked sad. "That's too bad. I can't seem to find the right one for me, either," she said. "I'd like to have a kitten, but with my travels, I don't think I can. I visit my grandchildren often, you know. What would I do with a cat while I was away?"

David wished his only problem was what to do with a pet when he wasn't around.

Why, if he had a pet, he'd find someone to take care of it when he was away. Some other kid who didn't have a pet. Some kid like—a flash of light went off in his brain.

"What if we shared the kitten?" The suggestion popped out of his mouth. Before Mrs. Palmer could answer, he explained his plan.

"The kitten would live with you, and I'd come to play with it and take care of it while you were away!" He held his breath, waiting for her to digest his plan.

Mrs. Palmer stuck out her hand. "It's a deal!" she said. "Now, let's pick out our kitten."

They headed for the kitten playpen at the front of the store and sat down in the middle. Pretty soon, kittens of all colors were clambering over them as if they were jungle gyms. After playing with the kittens for a while, they chose a gray and black tabby with bright green eyes and a purr as loud as a lion's.

"What should we call him?" asked Mrs. Palmer.

Cradling their new pet, David sunk his face into its silky fur. As he scratched underneath its chin, it purred like a revved-up motor. David had waited so long for this moment that the name had to be…

"Purr-fect!" he said.

 ## Comprehension Check

**1.** Why won't David's parents let him have a pet?

**2.** How does David feel about the stuffed animals and pet rock that his parents give him?

**3.** How does David solve his pet problem?

**4.** If David does a good job taking care of Mrs. Palmer's cat, do you think his parents will let him get his own pet? Why or why not?

# Saving Hairy Long Legs

*by Kim Childress*

"Cool!" Sara cried, pointing out the kitchen window. Curled up in the center of a huge, intricate, finely woven web was a yellow and black spider the size of a quarter. "Can he stay?"

Mom shuddered. "You and your bugs."

"Mom, spiders aren't bugs; they're arachnids. They have eight legs and two body parts, not six legs and three body parts like insects."

"Right. Just so long as that arachnid stays outside."

Sara named him Hairy Long Legs. Her friend, Jessie, came over and they thumbed through Sara's *Field Guide to Spiders,* trying to identify him.

"He kind of looks like this jumping spider," Sara said, "but he's too big, and he's got yellow bands on his legs."

"Maybe a wolf spider?" Jessie asked.

"He's big enough," Sara agreed, "but wolf spiders are brown and they don't spin webs. Here we go," she pointed to a picture of a garden spider, "that's him." She watched as Hairy ambushed a fly. "Look! Did you know spiders inject saliva that turns their prey's insides to mush? Then they suck everything out, like drinking a milk shake through a straw."

"Gross," Jessie said, but she pressed against the window next to Sara, watching Hairy consume the fly. Afterward, he crawled to the corner of the windowsill and curled into a tight little ball.

At sundown, Hairy stretched out in the center of his web, waiting patiently for his evening meal. Sara flipped on the porch lights to attract dinner. In a quick flash of yellow, legs barely touching the sticky threads, Hairy scurried over to a struggling moth that couldn't resist the light.

The next day a wild storm blew the web to shreds. Sara checked on Hairy as he hid in his corner, waiting for the rain to pass. By morning the reconstructed web stretched farther across the patio.

"Don't worry, Mom," Sara said, "the web doesn't touch the door. You can go outside."

"It's all right, dear," Dad said from behind the newspaper. "Confront your fears." Mom threw up her arms in surrender.

That night Sara switched on the porch light. "Mom! Dad! Come quick!" A giant green grasshopper was trapped tightly in Hairy's grasp. Its struggle completely unraveled the web.

Mom shivered. "Hideous! That's it. Tomorrow he goes."

"Oh, please can we wait one more night?" Sara begged. "So Jessie can stay over and watch him?"

Mom looked at Dad. "You're the executioner," he said, "or should I say exterminator?"

"Thanks a lot," she said. "One more night, Sara."

When Jessie arrived, Hairy still hadn't repaired his web. He had carried the grasshopper into the corner where he continued to gorge. "So what's your mom going to do to him?"

"Flyswatter," Sara said.

"Maybe the vacuum," Jessie suggested, "or the wadded up tissue and toilet flush."

"We can't let it happen!" Sara cried. She tossed and turned all night, wrestling the covers in her worry over Hairy. In the morning, she jostled Jessie awake and they crept downstairs.

The grasshopper's remains dangled in the still-tattered web. Hairy crouched in his corner.

"What are you going to do?" Jessie asked. She yawned and sat at the table.

"I'm smuggling him out of here. I'll take him to the woods."

"Mmmm," Jessie muttered, still half asleep.

Sara worked fast. With Cool Whip® container in hand, she tried scooping Hairy into the bowl. In self-defense, he opened up to full size and suddenly seemed enormous! Sara almost dropped the container. Hands shaking, she gently brushed him with the lid and pushed him in.

Holding the bowl as far away from her body as possible, Sara traversed the backyard to the edge of the woods.

Once there, she tried to set Hairy free in a patch of tall grass, but when she un-snapped the lid, he wouldn't budge. "Vamoose, Hairy. Scram! Get out of here!" Sara yelled. She thought about prodding him with a stick, but she might hurt him. She thought about picking him up, then changed her mind. She knew that garden spiders weren't dangerous, but Hairy still might bite her if she handled him. She tried shaking him out, but he stuck fast. She tapped the bottom of the bowl; finally, he fell out and scurried away.

Heart beating wildly, Sara raced back inside. She sat at the kitchen table next to Jessie and struggled to catch her breath. Before she said anything, Mom came down the stairs, shoe in hand.

"Say good-bye," she said.

"He's gone," Sara said, glancing at Jessie, who suddenly looked very much awake.

"Thank goodness," Mom said. "Well, how 'bout some breakfast?"

"Sure," Sara said. "Pancakes sound extra good, but no flies or grasshoppers, please."

Sara and Jessie smiled secretly at each other. Sara pictured Hairy scampering through the woods, building a new web just in time for lunch.

 ## Comprehension Check

1. How do Sara and Jessie identify the type of spider Hairy is?

2. How does Sara's mother feel about spiders? What makes you think so?

3. Do you think Jessie feels the way Sara does about spiders or the way Sara's mother feels about spiders? Why?

4. If you were Sara, would you save Hairy? If not, why? If so, how?

# Imaginary Journey

*by Sandy Steers*

Mrs. Lester stood before the classroom. She pushed her small, round glasses up her short, pointed nose and took a deep breath.

"Class, today we're going to learn about pelicans, but we're going to do it in a new way. We're going on an imaginary journey."

Maria Hijuelos sat up straighter in her seat. An imaginary journey? No textbooks? No worksheets? She hated trying to learn new things by reading about them. Lines of words marching like ants across a page made her head ache. Between the page and her brain, the ants did loop the loops. They didn't make much sense by the time they marched into her mind. But an imaginary journey? Maria smiled; she could make pictures in her mind. That sounded like her way of learning.

"Sit down, breathe deeply, and get completely relaxed," said Mrs. Lester in a melodic voice. "Now close your eyes and let your imagination take over."

Maria took a deep breath and closed her eyes. The tension she usually felt in school washed out her fingertips like water running down the drain.

"Feel your body getting lighter, as if it weighed only eight pounds," said Mrs. Lester. "Feel your body rounding into an oblong shape, almost like an egg tipped on its side. You are four feet long and covered with white and brown feathers. Stretch out your arms and feel them as strong wings, each over three feet long."

In her mind, Maria's arms morphed into long, strong wings.

"Rub your face against your wing. Does it feel soft and a little bit prickly?"

Maria shivered as her imaginary wing tickled her cheek.

"Comb between your wing feathers with your long, pointed beak. Feel how nice it is to scratch that itch on the tip of your left wing. Notice the flexible pouch on the lower half of your beak. You are a pelican!"

I am a pelican! Maria thought. Now what?

"Look down." Mrs. Lester's honey-smoothe voice answered Maria's unspoken question. "You are standing on webbed feet and short legs. Feel the wet, cool rocks under the pads of your flat feet. Can you see other pelicans nearby? You can't talk, so nod a greeting to them."

Maria nodded, imagining pelicans nodding all over the classroom, and grinned.

"Take a look at the world around you. You are on a tiny island of rocks. Hear the waves lapping against the rocks. The sun is getting low and the empty feeling in your stomach tells you it's time to search for dinner.

"Stand up tall and spread your wings to their full width. With your feet together, do little hops forward until you can leap into the air. What does it feel like to be airborne? Feel the breeze flowing past as your wings flap slowly through the air. Catch an air current and spiral up, up, up until you are a mile above the ground. What does the ocean look like from such height?"

To Maria, the ocean looked like a wrinkled blue sheet spread over a vast, deep bed.

"Drift down now, closer to the earth. Fold your wings and feel yourself plummet toward the water. Right before you reach the surface, start gently flapping to soar high once more. Pick up speed until you're flying over 25 miles per hour; then stretch out your wings and glide."

Maria glided toward the sea. Wind played with her feathers. The sun warmed her back.

"As you near your favorite hunting spot in the bay, drop down gradually and let your round belly skim right above the water's surface. Feel the cool mist rising off the waves, touching your chest feathers. Your wing tips brush near the water, but do not touch it.

"Now pull higher into the air and look down to spot fish with your excellent vision. When you spot one, fold your wings halfway and drop headfirst into the water. Smash into the water with enough force to stun fish up to six feet beneath you. But don't worry, you won't get hurt! The air pockets under the skin of your chest will protect you."

Maria almost gasped as she plunged into the water. It reminded her of the time she dove from the high dive into the community pool.

"With your head underwater, use your expandable throat pouch as a net to scoop up the stunned fish," said Mrs. Lester.

Maria brought her thoughts back to the ocean. She could easily picture the pelican's great, drooping pouch filling with fish.

"Pop up to the surface with your full pouch. Notice how it feels when your pouch is stretched to hold as much as three gallons of water. Tip your beak down to drain out the excess water. Then tip your head back to gulp down the fish. Swallow them whole."

Maria gulped and rubbed her stomach, then remembered that pelicans couldn't do that. No hands!

"As you float on the water's surface, see how you bob around because your air pockets make you buoyant. Feel that nice fullness in your stomach. It's sunset now. Time to go home. Pull yourself aloft and feel the water drip from your feet. Fly serenely back to your rocky island home.

"As you approach, notice that many other pelicans have already settled in for the night. You land a tad clumsily and tip over on one wing as you hit the rocks. Oh well, no one was watching! Waddle over to your buddy and nod a silent good-night.

"As you feel yourself drifting off to sleep, bring yourself back into your human body and open your eyes."

Maria opened her eyes and blinked. She could hardly believe she was in a classroom, not sitting atop a rock by the sea. She remembered everything she'd learned about the pelican. Maybe Mrs. Lester could help her turn every lesson into an imaginary journey!

## Comprehension Check

1. What kind of journey is Maria taking?

2. How does a pelican catch fish?

3. Maria finds it easier to learn from an imaginary journey that lets her make pictures in her mind. What kinds of learning activities do you find easier?

4. If you could be any animal for a day, which one would you choose? Why?

# What the Animals Knew

*by Kim T. Griswell*

*They say that animals have a kind of sixth sense that tells them things people don't know—like this person is nice, this one likes cats but not dogs, or something bad is about to happen. Mother claims this is rubbish. "They're nothing but dumb animals, Amanda," she says. She barely tolerates the three cats I've raised from kittens, and she turned away the stray pup that once sniffed its way to our door. But Mother is wise in many things, so when she said that animals were dumb, I believed her. Until the morning of April 18, 1906.*
—From the journal of Amanda Wyatt

I awakened early, as is my habit, pulled on thick stockings, stuffed my feet into my boots to protect them from the cold tiled floor, and clomped into the kitchen to light a fire in the woodstove. Later, Mother would awaken to fry savory bacon in an iron skillet and whip pancake batter with a wire whisk. But before the sun crested the eastern hills and breakfast filled my belly, there was work to do.

First, I needed to sweep the chapel and light the candles. Mother always led morning devotions in the tiny building outside the main house. It was a quiet, peaceful time of day. This day, I left the double doors open as I went about my chores. The spring air was strangely still, as if the wind held its breath as it entered the valley.

Outside, I heard cattle lowing. A deep, mournful sound, unusual for this time of day. I swept briskly, mixing bits of dried grass and crumbling clods of dirt. The air smelled of earth and dust and something strange, like a storm just before lightning strikes.

Just as I whisked the dirt out the front door, two little birds darted into the chapel and headed for the rafters.

"Oh, no!" I thought. "Mother will be angry if these birds interrupt her morning meditation."

I tried to shoo them down with the broom, but they'd set their tiny claws into the wood like nails hammered into planks. They would not be shooed.

Next, my three striped cats bolted through the door, one after another, and hid under three different pews.

"What is going on?" I bent down and peeked under the back bench. "What are you hiding from under there?" I asked. "Did you get into Mother's cream again?"

The cats usually mewed a soft greeting, but today they crouched still and silent as the morning air.

A strange yellow mutt followed. I thought I'd found the troublemaker until he too squeezed beneath a bench and began to tremble.

The last to arrive was a hummingbird, which buzzed down from a nearby apple tree and darted like a bee through the door. It hovered near the candles, its tiny wings fluttering too fast to see.

What was I to do? If Mother found this menagerie of animals here she'd send me to my room for a week!

I poked at the cats and the yellow dog, trying to budge them from beneath the benches. It did no good. I waved my hand at the hummingbird; it moved a few feet but did not head for the open door.

As I stared out the door, I saw that the sun had burst over the hills, turning them silver and gold. Light filled the doorway and waxed the wooden floor to a warm glow. I realized that it was time to light the candles. My hand shook a bit as I put match to wick, for I knew that Mother would be here within minutes. I could already see the scowl of displeasure she would give me.

Then something rocked the chapel; it shook as if it had been butted by mad bulls. The birds shook on their perch in the rafters. The hummingbird buzzed across the room. A rumbling tremor then knocked me to my knees. As I tried to rub away the throbbing pain, a third and fourth tremor caused the candles to fall from their silver sticks.

I struggled to my feet, rushing to stamp out the wicks before the flames could catch the floor afire. Then I rolled under a bench to join one of the cats as the floor pitched like the deck of a rolling ship.

At last the rocking and rumbling stopped. The yellow light streaming through the door was filled with dust.

One by one, the animals emerged from hiding. They left as they'd come: two birds, a trio of cats, a strange yellow dog, and a single hummingbird.

They knew, I thought. They knew! I heard my mother's voice in my head saying, "They're nothing but a bunch of dumb animals," and I smiled. Not dumb. Not dumb at all.

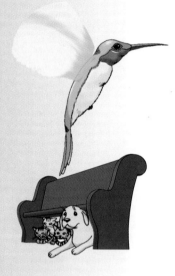

##  Comprehension Check

**1.** What kind of attitude does Amanda's mother have toward animals?

**2.** What is Amanda's morning job?

**3.** What natural disaster occurs in the story? How do you know?

**4.** Amanda's mother thinks that animals are dumb, and Amanda decides that they are not dumb. Do you think animals are dumb? Why or why not?

# Wild Horse of the Oregon Dunes

*by Shirley Nelson*

The black mare stopped chewing beach grass and lifted her head. Her keen ears heard the sounds of other horses—eating, swishing their tails, moving their feet. As she started to lower her head again, something caught her attention, and she paused, still as a statue. Sounds and smells of humans drifted toward her on the breeze. Wranglers had come to round up the herd of horses that grazed among the sand dunes.

The skittish mare moved farther away from the herd, breathing heavily, her nostrils flaring. The wranglers rode closer and tried to form the grazing horses into a group, heading them away from the ocean. With a shout, one man spotted her, gesturing wildly to the other wranglers. As he spurred his horse to give chase, the mare dug her hooves deep into the sand, and her muscular haunches propelled her away from her pursuers. She tossed her mane and careered toward the ocean.

Without saddle or rider, the mare could move much faster in the soft sand. She quickly outpaced her pursuers and looked for a place to hide. The dunes offered virtually unlimited cover for an animal that knew every twist and turn of this varied oceanside habitat. She ducked between the wind-carved hills and plunged into a manzanita thicket. Once she lost the wrangler's scent, she knew she had left him behind. Sides heaving, she climbed to the top of a dune to watch from afar. She whinnied into the sea air as the men rounded up the last few horses and turned their steeds toward home.

Almost all black with a flowing mane and a tail that brushed the ground, she stood a little over 15 hands tall. With her shiny coat and thick, flowing mane, she could have been named Beauty. With a small white star on her forehead, she could have been called Sea Star. The men who tried to catch her said she could run like the wind; they called her Windy. She was a mixture of Morgan, Percheron, and Mustang. From her Morgan ancestors came her intelligence, speed, and chance for longevity; she would probably live a long life. Her Percheron forebears gave her strength, a broad body, and hard, medium-sized hooves, which helped her move quickly in the sand. From the Mustang came her wild nature and love of freedom.

As the years passed, the black horse lived alone among the dunes and ran along the seashore. She shied away from other horses, knowing that their company meant probable capture. She lived free and wild, contentedly blending in with the natural environment around her.

Spring skies were often gray, torn by wind and flooded with rain. Whales spouted offshore on their biannual migration. Seagulls called above the roar of the surf. Summer brought fog, sunshine, and occasional winds that whipped her mane about her head. Autumn brought balmy days and beautiful sunsets. Winter blew in violent storms, torrential rain, and pounding waves. She sheltered under trees or on the leeward side of a boulder or sand dune to stay out of the wind. She fed on beach grass and leaves from bushes and trees. She drank from clear lakes and sparkling streams.

Sometimes people invaded her wild domain. She watched them riding horses along the beach. She stared as they picnicked in the shadows of the dunes. If they turned to stare back, she flared her nostrils and raced away. Those who tried to catch her found themselves chasing air.

For about 30 years, she lived her free, wild life. She was now more than 70 years old in people years. Her joints began to stiffen, and movement became painful. Each day's run felt harder than the last. On a cold day in April, she could not get up at all. When people walking in the dunes stumbled upon her, she could not clamber to her feet, wheel, and run away. Soon, her pain began to ease. The sound of the waves shushing

against the shore faded. The ocean breeze kissed her cheek. She closed her eyes and slept.

So the wild black mare died, old and weary, yet still proud and free. Some say her spirit still haunts the dunes near Coos Bay, Oregon. A wild whinny heard on a moonlit night might be the sound of the wind whipping through the hemlocks, or it might be the sound of a ghostly mare still enjoying her freedom.

##  Comprehension Check

**1.** Where does this story take place?

**2.** Why do you think the black mare heads for freedom?

**3.** How does the author describe the mare?

**4.** If you saw a wild horse, would you want to capture it or would you let it run free? Why?

# Smoking Mountain

*a Native American folktale retold by Agnes M. Bierbaum*

On May 18, 1980, 11-year-old John Tillikish squatted in front of the television, waiting for news from the scientists watching the bulge grow on the side of Mount St. Helens. The volcano had been rumbling and spouting ash and steam for months but had not yet fully erupted. Members of John's extended family had left their homes in the shadow of the mountain weeks before. Aunts, uncles, cousins, and grandparents were stuffed into his aunt's house in Portland like sardines in a can.

As John waited for news, his grandfather wandered into the room.

"Loowit is restless," he said.

John nodded. The legend of Mount St. Helens had been passed down by the Cowlitz tribe for generations. The elders said that the mountain slept for hundreds of years only to awaken in a rage. It spewed out fire and ash that destroyed forests, rivers, wildlife, humans, and dwellings for miles around. The Cowlitz tribe named the mountain "Lawelatla," or "one from whom smoke comes." The Klickitats called it "Tah-One-Lat-Clah," or "Fire Mountain."

"Grandfather, would you tell me the story again?"

The elderly man smiled, then nodded.

John leaned back on a pillow and closed his eyes as his grandfather's deep voice washed over him.

Once there lived an ugly old witch named Loowit, who guarded a sacred fire burning near a natural rock bridge over the Columbia River. This was the only fire in the world, so it had to be kept burning. Loowit took her job seriously and never failed to keep the fire alive.

The Great Spirit Sahale called to Loowit one day and said, "You have been a faithful guardian of the sacred fire. As a reward for your service, I will give you eternal life."

Loowit thanked Sahale for his generous gift, but pleaded with him, "Please, Great Spirit, I do not want to live forever as an ugly old witch."

Sahale took pity on Loowit and turned her into a young woman as beautiful as the sun, moon, and stars. Then the troubles began.

Two brothers fell madly in love with the beautiful Loowit. One was chief of the Klickitats and the other the chief of the Multnomahs. Loowit could not decide between the two brothers, so they fought for her attention. They burned forests and villages, and ravished the land around them.

The Great Spirit was angered. He shouted to the chiefs, "Stop destroying the land, or I will punish both of you!"

The chiefs did not listen. Each day brought more destruction. The Great Spirit became so angry that he turned them into mountains where they stood. The tall, proud, handsome chief of the Multnomahs became Mount Hood. As the Klickitat chief changed, he hung his head and wept for his lost love; thus he took the form of Mount Adams.

Even as mountains, the rivals continued to throw stones and fire at each other. The rocks they threw choked the Columbia River below them and caused it to narrow at certain places as it flowed through the valley.

Loowit, who loved the earth, was saddened by the devastation the chiefs brought to the land while they fought to win her love. She told the Great Spirit, "I no longer want to live as a beautiful young woman. This war between the chiefs must end."

The Great Spirit was compassionate. He did not return Loowit to her former state as an ugly old woman, but chose to change her into a perfectly formed mountain, Mount

St. Helens. A cloak of white snow made her even more dazzling. He placed this majestic mountain between the quarreling Mount Hood and Mount Adams to keep peace.

"Vancouver…Vancouver…this is it!" a voice crackled out of the television. John opened his eyes and watched the television screen. The long-awaited eruption had come. His mouth fell open. He turned to look at his grandfather. "Loowit still keeps the sacred fire alive," the old man said.

 **Comprehension Check**

1. What happens at the beginning of this story?

2. Why does the Great Spirit turn the two chiefs and Loowit into mountains?

3. Why do you think Native Americans made up tales like the one about Mount St. Helens?

4. If you had to make up a tale to explain why volcanoes erupt, what story would you tell?

# The Tale of the Broom's Sticks

*an Aesop fable retold by Beverly Swerdlow Brown*

Once upon a time in a small village in China lived a tailor named Wu Chen. He had three sons named Wu Shing, Wu Jun, and Wu Lei. One day, Wu Chen called his children together.

"My sons," he said, "I have worked hard through the years. Now I wish to spend my remaining days resting in the shade of the trees. I am giving the tailor shop to you."

Lei stepped forward. "Thank you, Father," he said. "My brothers and I hope that we can live up to your wise teachings."

Wu Chen smiled. "How wonderful it will be to see my sons working together."

Shing picked up some cloth. "I will design the garments," he said excitedly.

"I will cut the patterns," added Jun happily.

"And I will sew the pieces of cloth," said Lei eagerly.

"Excellent," said Wu Chen, nodding. "You have made me very happy."

The very next day, the three brothers learned that the emperor had offered a prize of 100 gold pieces for a wedding gown worthy of his daughter, the princess.

"Our fortune will be assured!" exclaimed Shing.

"We will become known throughout the city," said Jun.

"Everyone will buy our fine clothing," rejoiced Lei.

Wu Chen moved closer. "I must journey to the city to buy more cloth, but I will return tomorrow. I know that you will work well together, my sons."

After his father left, Shing picked up some paper. I should win the prize because I will design the garment, he thought. He quickly drew some sketches of a beautiful wedding dress.

"Show us what you have drawn," said Lei.

Shing hid the paper behind his back with a smile.

"This design is not worthy enough for the gown of a princess," he said. "I will not embarrass you by asking you to help me make my gown. I will make this gown myself." An arrogant gleam sparkled in his eyes.

Jun noticed the hard glint in his brother's eye and became suspicious. I should win the prize because I will cut the pattern, he thought, so he said, "Brother, I am certain that your design would bring a smile like the rising sun to the princess's face. I fear that my humble skills will not allow me to cut a pattern that would be worthy of such a design. So I will make a gown myself." A smile spread across his face as he contemplated the riches that would soon be his.

Lei spotted the sly edge of Jun's smile, and he became suspicious. I should win the prize because I will sew the fine stitches, he thought.

"Brothers," said Lei, "I fear that the stitches I sew will not be fine and delicate enough for your gowns, so I will make a gown of my own." He imagined a gown with embroidery so rich that no princess could refuse it, and his chest puffed out with pride.

The brothers worked all through the night, each certain that his gown would be chosen by the emperor. When the sun crested over the mountain beyond their village, Wu Chen returned to find his sons asleep at their tables.

"Show me your gown," said Wu Chen.

"Father," said Shing, "my design was not worthy of my brothers' fine work, so I have made a gown of my own." He held up a gown that looked nothing like his beautiful design. The sleeves were too long; the shoulders were too wide; scraggly stitches puckered the fine red satin.

Wu Chen shook his head, barely able to conceal his consternation. "Jun?"

"Father," said Jun, "my pattern was not worthy of my brothers' fine work, so I have

made a gown of my own." He held up a plain gown with long, uneven stitches.

Hardly able to hide his dismay, Wu Chen furrowed his grizzled brows. "Lei?"

"Father," said Lei, "my stitches were not worthy of my brothers' fine work, so I have made a gown of my own." He held up a gown with fine, delicate stitches, but the pieces did not fit together properly.

No longer able to disguise his disappointment, Wu Chen sadly shook his head. "As of this moment, I do not even see the beginning of a gown that would please the emperor."

The brothers' faces crinkled in shame, but they said nothing.

Wu Chen fetched a broom from the doorway and removed three sticks.

"Shing," he said, "can you break this stick?"

"Of course," replied Shing, snapping it in half.

"What about you, Jun?" asked Wu Chen. "Can you break a stick too?"

"Easily," answered Jun, snapping one in half.

"Can you do the same, Lei?" asked Wu Chen.

"Certainly, Father," replied Lei, snapping the last stick in half.

The sons looked at each other, puzzled.

Wu Chen held the broken sticks in his hands. "It seems easier to stand alone, but alone, each stick breaks easily."

Wu Chen picked up the broom.

"Now," he said, "break all the bound sticks at one time!"

Each brother took a turn, but no one could do it.

"Though a stick alone can be easily broken, together the sticks are too strong to break."

The brothers looked at one another and nodded.

"We understand, Father," said Lei.

"We have wasted time being greedy," said Jun.

"Now it is too late to make a beautiful gown, Father," said Shing.

Wu Chen nodded. "But it is never too late to learn a good lesson."

And from that day forward, Wu Shing, Wu Jun, and Wu Lei designed and cut and sewed each garment together, and soon their work was favored throughout the city.

## Comprehension Check

1. What part of the tailoring process does each brother do best?

2. Why do the three brothers decide to make separate gowns for the princess?

3. What lesson do the brothers learn from the broom's sticks?

4. Fables often teach lessons. What other fables have you read or heard, and what lessons do they teach?

# Ashi, the Stonecutter

*a Japanese folktale retold by Jeanne Mayo*

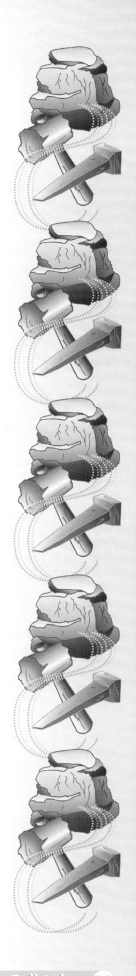

Tuesday after Tuesday and all the days in between, the stonecutter, Ashi, chipped and chiseled at a great stone, cutting it into smaller blocks. All day long he chiseled and chipped. Every day was the same, until one day as he stared out the window of his damp and dreary hut, Ashi spoke to the wind.

"Ah, I am the most powerless of creatures," he said. "How I wish that I could be a fat, rich, powerful man who sits all day upon a sofa covered in silk."

With a whooshing swirl of wind, his hands grew plump and smooth. He sat not in his dismal hut, but upon a silken sofa in a fine home. Servants bowed before him as they brought him platters filled with fruits and nuts and sweets.

Day after day, he slurped plums and watched travelers pass by his open window, until one windy day Ashi saw the people bow as a king passed by.

"Humph! That king has more power than I do," said Ashi. "All the people must bow to him, not just his servants. I wish that I were a king."

With a whooshing swirl of wind, a crown of purple jewels slipped upon his head; his wish had been granted once again. Day after day, King Ashi traveled the countryside. Everywhere he went, people hurried outside to stare and bow as he passed. Ashi nodded regally, basking in their attention, but the hot sun soon drove them inside.

"Humph! The sun has more power than I do," said Ashi. "They are at its mercy every day. I wish that I were the blazing sun."

With a whooshing swirl of wind, Ashi flew into the sky and became the sun. He beamed down upon the earth. He sent warmth to the tiny buds in the spring, and when he grew weary of this, he shone in one spot, torching the land and blistering the skin of the people below.

"I have power over all, for nothing can match my strength," Ashi gloated.

One day while he was withering yet another plum tree, a cloud blocked his view. "Who dares to block the almighty sun?" he roared. As he watched, power-less to move the cloud, it sent welcome rain to the parched plum tree.

"Humph! That little cloud has more power than I do," said Ashi. "I wish that I were a cloud."

A whooshing swirl of wind transformed him into a cloud. Day after day, Ashi marveled in his new power; he sent rain and shade to the plum trees and flooded the rivers with currents that washed away anything in their paths. Then one day he noticed something disturbing.

"What is that large rock doing? It is still among my river currents." Try as he might, with rain upon rain and mighty swirling floods, Ashi could not move the rock.

"Humph! That rock has more power than I do," said Ashi. "I wish that I were that rock."

A whooshing swirl of wind appeared and Ashi became a boulder. Day after day he stood, still and steady. The river washed around him, but he did not move; boys raced from the river's edge to touch his hard sides. Thus he stayed until one day an old stonecutter waded out and climbed upon his great surface. The stonecutter began to chip and chisel, and flakes of the rock fell into the water around him.

"Can a mere stonecutter have such tremendous power?" Ashi asked himself. "If so, then that is what I wish to be."

With a whooshing swirl of wind, Ashi was transformed back into the stone-

cutter he was before. Tuesday after Tuesday and all the days in between, he smiled and whistled as he worked.

## Comprehension Check

1. Why does Ashi wish to be something other than a stonecutter at the beginning of this tale?

2. What five things does Ashi become?

3. Why do you think Ashi is never satisfied with what he becomes?

4. If you could be anyone or anything you wished, who or what would you choose to be? Why?

# How the Mosquito Came to Alaska

*a Tlingit Indian legend retold by Elizabeth Silverthorne*

Long ago Chief Raven gave the people of the North the sun and the moon, and fire to cook their food and keep them warm. This mischievous Raven sometimes played tricks on the people, but usually he helped them.

Only one thing spoiled their happiness. They lived in terror of the giant cannibal. Often when they were singing and dancing around their bonfires, they could feel his evil, penetrating eyes watching them from the darkness.

One day, two young brothers decided that they must journey from their coastal village to the mountains to hunt goats. Their father had fallen from a cliff the previous year during a hunt. Their mother vowed not to comb her hair while the boys were away so that they would not be "combed" from the perilous cliffs, but she knew no ritual to protect them from the cannibal. Perhaps Chief Raven would protect them.

While the brothers ate their lunch of bread and cheese, they talked about Raven. Sometimes, they knew, he looked like a chieftain; other times he looked like a bird. Suddenly they heard a great whirring sound, and Chief Raven appeared, wearing a cape made of bird feathers.

"Why have two young boys journeyed so far from the village?" he boomed.

When the boys explained, Raven nodded. "You show great courage for boys so young. But courage will not save you from the giant cannibal."

"We have our bows and arrows," said the elder brother. "If the giant cannibal tries to eat us, we will shoot him!" The youngest brother nodded eagerly.

"Ha!" Raven laughed. His feathered cape shook. "Arrows cannot harm the giant cannibal, but I will give you four things to help you."

He handed the eldest a bundle of sticks and a bag made of skin, filled with oil. To the youngest, Raven gave a small bag of stones and a skin bag filled with water.

The brothers looked at one another. They wondered how sticks and stones and water and oil could help them against the ferocious giant cannibal.

The elder brother whispered, "I wish he would give us bows and arrows."

Raven's black eyebrows drew together. "Go!" he growled. "I have given you enough!"

As the boys ran, they bent low, searching the ground for hoofprints. After a few hours, they were stiff and exhausted; every step became painful, but they kept on.

"It's getting dark," the eldest said.

His younger brother pointed to the sky, "But the sun is only halfway down. It's a giant shadow. Something must be behind us!"

They whirled to see the grinning face and long fangs of the giant cannibal. His huge, hulking shape blotted out the sunlight.

The terrified brothers forgot their exhaustion; they ran as they had never run before. Not even in the village races had their legs moved so fast, but the cannibal covered ground ten times faster.

"These sticks are slowing me down," cried the eldest. As he threw the bundle of sticks away, they flew in all directions. Everywhere they touched the earth, forests sprang up.

The trees hid the boys for a few minutes and obscured their view of the giant. Soon, though, they heard the giant tromping through the forest, crunching trees underfoot.

The younger brother cried, "These stones are too heavy!" As he flung the bag of stones away, they flew far and wide. Everywhere they touched the earth, mountains and hills sprang up.

"Hurrah!" shouted the elder brother. "Even a giant can't see over those mountains."

He started to sit on a rock, when his younger brother shouted.

"Look!" The young brother pointed to the tallest mountain peak where the cannibal stood, scanning the ground. I can run faster without this bag of water banging against my leg, thought the younger brother, so he tossed the skin behind him. The bag burst open and a huge fountain splashed up.

Everywhere water drops touched the earth, rivers and lakes appeared. "I'm glad you threw the water behind us instead of in front of us," gasped the elder brother. "I'll throw away this bag of oil as well. I can run faster without it."

"No," warned his younger brother. "Raven will be angry if we waste his last gift."

"All right," grumbled the elder, "but it may be one of Raven's tricks."

In the distance, they saw smoke curling above the roofs of the village huts. If they could keep out of the giant's clutches for a few more minutes, they would be safe.

The giant's footsteps thundered in their ears. The elder brother felt the giant's hot breath on his neck. A rough claw closed around him. It squeezed into a fist and lifted him off the ground.

"Throw the oil on him!" shouted his brother.

The eldest hurled the skin bag of oil into the giant's face with all his strength. The bag hit the giant's forehead; oil cascaded down his face and oozed over his body. As he reached up to rub his eyes, the struggling boy slipped through his greasy fist. The brothers stumbled toward the village with the cannibal right behind them.

Just as his hairy claws reached out to grasp them, a great blast of wind knocked the boys off their feet. Raven dropped down between them and the giant. "You have caused enough trouble!" he thundered as he touched a feather to the oil on the giant's body.

Instantly the giant turned into a cloud of smoke and ash. As the ash rained down, the giant's gruff voice spread across the village, "May my ashes remain to plague you forever!"

The villagers came running. In a few minutes, nothing was left of the giant except gray ashes. Then the ashes began to stir. They rose from the ground with a loud buzzing sound. The two brothers felt sharp, little stings on their faces, arms, and legs.

The people of the North saw that the cannibal's ashes had become tiny insects with wings. His curse had come true. They would forevermore be plagued by the endless mosquitoes of the air.

The two young brothers grew up to be honored hunters, but every time a mosquito bit one of them, he would sigh and say, "The giant cannibal is still trying to eat us!"

 **Comprehension Check**

1. Why do the two brothers journey beyond the protection of the village?

2. What four things does Raven give the boys and how does each thing help them?

3. Why do you think the Tlingit people created a tale to explain where mosquitoes came from?

4. Native American tribes often have legends that explain the natural world. What other tales of this kind have you heard or read?

# The Chalk Mark

*by Joanne Mattern*

Margaret Hayes sat up in her narrow bed. There was too much noise around her to sleep. Everyone in the crowded steerage quarters was shouting and rushing around.

"What's going on?" the ten-year-old asked a woman as she rushed by.

The woman smiled. "We're in America. The ship is pulling into New York Harbor."

Margaret could hardly believe her ears. She grinned back at the woman. Like Margaret, she and the others on the ship had left Ireland for a new life in America.

Margaret reached into the basket at the head of her bed. It contained everything she owned—two dresses, some underwear, a pair of shoes, a book, and a comb for her hair. She decided to put on her pretty dress, not the plain one she'd been wearing all through the journey. It wasn't every day a girl arrived in America!

Before she went up on deck, Margaret pulled out her handkerchief and blew her nose. The crowded steerage quarters seemed to provide the perfect environment for sickness to spread. She had caught a nasty cold during the journey and had been sneezing and coughing for days. Margaret made her way up the narrow staircase. She was happy to leave the hot, noisy, smelly steerage quarters behind for the fresh air on deck.

Margaret had no trouble spotting her 16-year-old brother, Patrick, on deck. His height helped him stand out in the crowd.

"We're here at last!" Patrick exclaimed when he saw her. "Look at all the buildings!"

Margaret followed his pointing finger. She gasped. New York City was bigger than she had ever imagined. It was nothing like their tiny village at home in Ireland.

Patrick and Margaret had been on their own ever since their parents had died. Patrick's friends had told him stories about the opportunities in America. After saving every penny for several years, Margaret and Patrick finally had enough money to make the ocean voyage to the New World.

Margaret and her brother followed the crowd onto a barge. A few minutes later, they pulled up to a landing slip and were led to the Main Building.

"This must be Ellis Island," Patrick said. "It's time to get inspected." He must have noticed the fear in her eyes because he put a hand on her shoulder and whispered into her ear. "This is a new country, Maggie. A new world. It's a land of freedom and opportunity. We must trust our new country. Do you understand?"

Margaret nodded. Patrick's friends had told him stories about Ellis Island. Here, most immigrants were examined to make sure they were well enough to enter the country.

Margaret and Patrick lined up with the others and walked into the immigration station. Then they filed up a big flight of stairs. Margaret held tightly to her basket of belongings. What if the inspectors didn't like the way she looked? Her heart pounded nervously.

Margaret could feel her chest tightening and her nose running as she stepped up to the first inspector. Suddenly, she broke into a fit of coughing. "I don't like the sound of those lungs," the man muttered. He marked a big letter *P* on her coat with a piece of chalk. "Go wait over there," he told her.

"But sir—" Margaret said.

"She's my sister," Patrick added.

"Go wait over there," the inspector repeated sharply. He gave her a gentle push. Margaret stumbled to a group of immigrants waiting behind a rope. Each one had a letter marked on his or her coat.

Margaret had heard stories of immigrants who were sent back home because they

were too sick to stay in America. Perhaps that was the doctor's intention. Margaret looked around at the others crowded behind the rope. They looked like frightened rabbits. A girl standing nearby glanced nervously around, as if checking to see if anyone was looking. No one besides Margaret was paying any attention to her. She quickly shrugged her coat off her shoulders and stuffed it into her basket. Then she walked over to the rope separating the sick immigrants. The girl took a deep breath and ducked under the rope. She pushed into the crowd and hurried into the next room, the same room Patrick had disappeared into.

"Should I do the same thing?" Margaret asked herself. "I just have a cold." A cold certainly didn't seem like a legitimate reason to keep anyone out of a country. It wasn't fair.

Margaret started to take off her coat, then she stopped. No. Patrick had told her to trust this new country; that's what she would do. She would trust that the doctors would know a cold when they saw one and that they would be fair.

After a long wait behind the rope, someone came to take her to another room. There, a doctor with kind eyes did a careful examination. He scribbled notes on a file, then smiled at Margaret.

"Young lady, you have a cold," he said.

Margaret grinned. "I know!" She sneezed.

The doctor handed her a tissue. Then he dusted the chalk mark from her coat.

"Welcome to America!" he said.

A few minutes later, Margaret called to her brother across a big room.

"Margaret!" he hurried to her side. "I thought I would never see you again. I thought you would be too scared to talk to the doctors."

"I just remembered what you told me. I trusted that a land of freedom and opportunity wouldn't send me away because of a cold and a chalk mark," Margaret said.

"That's my girl," Patrick said as he gave his sister a quick hug.

 ## Comprehension Check

**1.** Why are Margaret and Patrick traveling to America?

**2.** Why does Margaret decide not to take off her coat and slip away like the other girl does?

**3.** What do you think the *P* on Margaret's coat stands for?

**4.** Most American families emigrated from another country. Did your family? If so, from which country or countries did your ancestors come?

# Happy Birthday, Ben!

*by Kim T. Griswell*

Masey wandered along the street toward Boston's Old City Hall Plaza, drawn by the statue there. She looked up at the familiar face she'd seen on wrinkled hundred-dollar bills, in history books, and on Web sites. It was the face of one of her heroes: Benjamin Franklin.

Ben was a book lover, just like Masey. Whenever he got a spare bit of money, he bought books and consumed them as quickly as cotton candy. She'd come to the statue today for one reason—to wish Ben a happy birthday. Kneeling down, she opened her lunchbox and carefully unwrapped the candy-sprinkled cupcake inside. She scrambled in the pocket of her parka, then withdrew the pack of matches her mom had given her to light the candle.

Removing her fur-lined gloves, she ignored the cold January air that bit her fingers and struck the match. Shielding the single candle with one shaking hand, she lit it with the other. The wick burned merrily, dancing a birthday jig in the breeze.

Masey stood and lifted the cupcake toward the statue. She imagined that she saw a gleam in the crinkly eyes and a smile curving the weathered lips. "Happy Birthday, Ben!" she said. As the words left her lips, a spiral of wind whipped around the candle, snuffing out its light.

"Hope you got your wish!" Masey said.

"Well, now, I think I did." A voice that crackled like melting ice came from the statue.

Masey dropped the cupcake and backed away. She could not be seeing what she thought she was seeing. That bronze head could not be turning. Those stiff knees could not be bending and popping like firecrackers, and Ben Franklin could not be bouncing down from the platform to stand beside her, grinning.

"I say, it's freezing out here." He rubbed his hands together, then stuffed them under his arms.

"It's always freezing in Boston in the middle of January," Masey said, though she wasn't sure why she was still standing here and not running for home as fast as her feet could carry her.

"Of course. January 17—my birthday. Always cold on my birthday. That's one of the reasons why I built the stove, you know." He smiled down at Masey.

"Stove?"

"Yes. Fireplaces were much too dangerous. And who could ever chop enough wood to feed their hunger? My iron furnace not only kept homes warmer, but it saved a lot of them from catching fire too."

"Hey, we have a Franklin stove in our house!" Masey said. "You invented that?"

Ben nodded. His smile was modest, but his eyes confident.

"Now, let me see." He pulled a pair of wire-rimmed glasses from his waist pocket and perched them on his heavy, pointed nose. Then he peered up at a billboard.

"Got milk?" he read. He took off his glasses and polished the lenses. "Must be something wrong with these, though till now they've worked quite well. Look." He held the glasses toward Masey. "It's really quite simple, you know. All I had to do was take two pairs of lenses and cut them in half. Then I put half of each lens in a single frame, and there you are! I can see up close as well as far away—with one pair of spectacles."

"Bifocals," Masey nodded. "Lots of folks have them now."

"Indeed?" Ben cocked his head to one side. "But what is this thing about milk? Surely the cows still graze on Boston Common. There should be no shortage of milk in such a great city."

Masey laughed. "The only animals grazing on Boston Common these days are tourists."

"Everything's so different." Ben shook his head.

He peered around him. "My old school used to stand around here somewhere. Did it burn?"

"No." Masey shook her head. "It is now in another neighborhood."

"Just as well. You know my father's house is not far from here." With that, Ben began to walk briskly out of the plaza. Masey grabbed her lunchbox and hurried after him.

At the corner of Washington and School streets, Ben clapped his hands. "Ah, I wonder if the bookseller's apprentices would know who I am."

The Old Corner Bookstore was one of Boston's oldest structures. Could Ben have really been there?

He leaned toward her and whispered. "Booksellers' apprentices used to loan me books to read. As long as I got them back in time for the shop to open the next morning, all was well.

"Clouds gather." He pointed to the sky. "We'd better hurry. Don't you think it odd that storms can travel one way, while their winds whip along in another?"

"I guess I never thought about it," Masey said. Her lunchbox banged against her knee as she tried to keep up with his increased pace.

"I once chased a whirlwind three-quarters of a mile trying to determine why storms fly thus. My horse wanted nothing more than to rear and run in the opposite direction!"

After a block, they turned onto Milk Street. Masey recognized the Old South Meeting House where the Boston Tea Party began. Ben stopped in front of it and stared across the street for a moment.

"My birthplace," he said.

"I know," Masey said. "We study your life in school now."

"Do you?" Ben looked surprised. "Well, if you would not be forgotten, as soon as you are dead and rotten, either write things worth reading, or do things worth the writing. Which of these did I do?"

Masey thought about some of Ben's inventions and discoveries: the Franklin Stove, bifocals, how he'd learned to plot the course of storms and proven that lightning is electricity. He'd also founded America's first circulating library so that people who couldn't afford to buy books could borrow them to read. She wondered if his experience with the booksellers' apprentices had given him the idea. He proposed the idea of daylight saving time, and, best of all, he'd written parts of the Declaration of Independence.

Masey reached out to take his hand.

"Both, Ben," Masey said. "You did both."

His smile widened. "Well, then, I can rest easy."

A cold wind whipped around the corner and plump, white flakes began to fall. Masey closed her eyes and stuck out her tongue to catch one. When she opened them and turned to Ben, he was gone.

"Happy Birthday, Ben," Masey whispered.

 ## Comprehension Check

**1.** What happens when Masey lights the birthday candle and wishes Ben a happy birthday?

**2.** What do Ben and Masey have in common?

**3.** When Masey says that Ben has both written things worth reading and done things worth writing about, to what is she referring?

**4.** If you could meet one historical figure, whom would you choose? Why?

# The Mystery Tulip

*by Ann Lenssen*

Hendrik opened the door as his grandfather trudged up the path. Their home filled the first floor of a windmill, with one large room serving as a kitchen, dining room, and living room and two sleeping cupboards built into the walls. Hendrik couldn't remember living anywhere else.

Grandfather sighed, "Meneer Visser says we pay him the final 500 guilders we owe for the windmill or he sells it to someone else."

"But Grootpapa, it's almost paid for and we have nowhere else to live!"

Grandfather's shoulders slumped. "We have sold the oxen and wagon already. There is nothing left to sell."

Hendrik twisted his ragged woolen cap. I'll be 13 in the spring, he thought. Then I will get a job in Amsterdam, but Meneer Visser will not wait. I must get some money now.

"I'm going for a walk, Grootpapa. Maybe I'll think of some way to help." On the main road, oxen pulled carts piled high with potatoes, onions, and cabbages, the last of the vegetable harvest. They bounced over ruts, heading for Amsterdam to market. The October wind felt chilly on Hendrik's cheeks. He pulled his cap lower and kept his head down to stay warm.

He stared vacantly at the rutted road until his gaze was arrested by a tulip bulb nestled in a deep depression. It must have fallen off a cart and rolled into the grass, Hendrik thought. It has been here awhile, as it already shows a green sprout in the center. Hendrik tucked it into his pocket. By the time he reached Amsterdam, he'd also found three potatoes and two onions.

As he rounded the corner of the central square, his eyes widened. An enormous painting advertised several tulips. One called Semper Augustus sold for 4,000 guilders at the last auction! This is insane, thought Hendrik. It's just a flower bulb.

Even so, he remembered the frenzied tulip auctions in Amsterdam last spring. The tulip craze started in France, where ladies of the court wore the *tulipa* as a status symbol.

Hendrik stared at the painting. One tulip, 2,000 guilders. Then he remembered the tulip in his pocket. His heart started to pound. What if?

He took a deep breath and headed for Lindenstraat, the tree-lined street of Amsterdam's open-air market. Stalls held strings of onions hung like bunches of bananas, piles of cabbage, and fresh herring from the sea. He barely glanced at them as he searched for the tulip vendors. There, at the far end! He wiped his sweaty palms on his jacket.

I'll just watch for a while, he decided. Each time a vendor held up a bulb, one person tried to outbid another. Hendrik listened as they paid for the bulbs with sacks of wheat, pounds of cheese, pigs, a silver cup, even a bed with bedding! The newspapers were correct, he realized, this is truly "tulipomania"!

Hendrik thought about his tulip bulb. How can I sell it when I don't even know what color it is? Customers want the fancy blossoms, the striped ones, the bright-colored ones. Then an idea blossomed.

He pulled the bulb from his pocket. "Folks, I have a special tulip bulb for sale."

"What color is it?" asked one customer.

"What's the name? Is it an Admiral? A Marvel? A Morillon?" another persisted.

"Everyone can buy those," chided Hendrik. "This is a mystery bulb. Plant it in your garden now, and you will have five months for your imagination to soar. What will it be? Perhaps a Laprock? Or even a Semper Augustus?"

Hendrik heard the customers gasp, then smile and nod.

"Yes! A mystery tulip!" said one. "It could be one of Holland's finest."

"It looks healthy," said another. "See the fresh, green sprout? It's ready for planting."

"What am I offered?" asked Hendrik.

"Three bushels of rye," shouted one woman.

"Two sheep," yelled a man.

"I will take only guilders,"' said Hendrik, "to pay a debt. Who will offer me guilders?"

A well-dressed man raised his hand. "One hundred guilders."

Another reached for the bulb. "Three hundred."

"This is a mystery bulb," reminded Hendrik. "Perhaps it will be the most amazing color ever!"

"I want it," said a woman in a velvet dress. "I will pay you six hundred guilders for it. I must have the mystery tulip!"

Hendrik took her bag of money and pressed the bulb into her outstretched hand. "Dear woman, you have made a wise choice. May this tulip bloom vividly for you in the spring!" A crowd gathered around her, and Hendrik started home, whistling.

 ## Comprehension Check

**1.** Why does Hendrik need to earn money?

**2.** What kinds of things are people willing to trade for tulip bulbs?

**3.** Why do you think the people who bid on Hendrik's tulip bulb are willing to pay so much for an unidentified bulb?

**4.** If you were in Hendrik's position, what would you do to help Grootpapa earn money?

# An Idea for Mr. Ford

*by Patricia McFadden*

Henry Ford seemed despondent.

"It's the depression," he complained as he stood with one foot propped on a wooden box, getting his shoes shined. "With so many people unemployed, the farmers can't sell their crops so they can't afford to buy my automobiles. They've been my best customers, so now I may have to start laying folks off in my manufacturing plants."

Even though he was just a 12-year-old shoeshine boy, Jasper knew about Mr. Ford. He knew that Mr. Ford's assembly line had changed the way cars were made and how much they cost. Cars used to be too expensive for farmers. Only rich folks could afford them. Mr. Ford made it possible for people like farmers to buy cars, but the Great Depression had made things hard for everyone, even the great Mr. Ford and his assembly-line workers.

"That's terrible!" Jasper exclaimed. "Say, why don't you help the farmers out? Other foot, please." He gestured toward Mr. Ford's left foot.

"What do you mean?"

Jasper began applying polish to Mr. Ford's left shoe, then picked up his buffing cloth.

"Well, if you could find a crop that you could use to make cars, you could pay the farmers for it. Then they'd have money to buy your cars. There, all done." He swiped his cloth across the shoe one last time. "Ten cents, please."

"Hmmm…not a bad idea," Mr. Ford admitted. "Unfortunately, I can't use carrots to build cars."

"Not carrots, but something like…oh, like…" Jasper's gaze fell on his can of shoe polish, "…like soybeans!" he exclaimed.

"Soybeans?"

"That's right, soybeans, or rather soybean oil. I have been trying it in my shoe polish. Maybe you could use it to make car paint or something."

"Soybeans. Interesting. I'll think about it." Mr. Ford dropped a quarter into Jasper's outstretched hand. "There's ten cents for the shine and 15 cents for the suggestion. Tell me, why are you trying to formulate your own shoe polish?"

"Store-bought polish isn't that good. Besides, I enjoy experimenting."

"I've always enjoyed experimentation myself. Perhaps you'll grow up to be an inventor like me." With a wink and a nod, he walked off with a thoughtful look on his face.

Jasper didn't see Henry Ford again for quite some time. Then, one day, he appeared with another gentleman.

"So, this is the young fellow who started it all?" the other man commented. "What's your name, son?"

"Jasper, sir. Jasper Peters," Jasper answered. What, he wondered, had he started, and how much trouble was it going to cause him?

"Well, Jasper, Mr. Ford tells me it was you who gave him the notion of using soybeans to make cars."

"It was just an idea," Jasper defended himself. "I didn't mean any harm."

"Harm!" exclaimed Mr. Ford. "My boy, it was a stroke of genius! We've already developed a car enamel using soybean oil, and my chemists are working on half a dozen other products. You've been a tremendous help. This gentleman is from my research and development department. He wanted to meet the bright young man with the big ideas."

"I'm pleased to meet you, sir!" Jasper wiped his right hand on the back of his pants

and held it out. "But I'm not sure why you'd want to meet me. All I did was tell Mr. Ford my idea."

The man who had revolutionized automobile production smiled. "My boy," he said, "never underestimate the value of a good idea."

## Comprehension Check

**1.** Why is Mr. Ford worried at the beginning of this story?

**2.** Why does Jasper suggest that Mr. Ford find a way to use soybeans in automobile manufacturing?

**3.** Besides making cars more inexpensive so that more people could buy them, how do you think Mr. Ford's invention of the automobile assembly line changed the world?

**4.** Although the shoeshine boy in the story is fictional, Henry Ford did use soybean oil to make car enamel. How do you think he came up with the idea to use plants in his automobiles?

# Bursting to Be Free

*by Kim T. Griswell*

When Anne first opened the colorful plaid diary on her 13th birthday, its blank pages gleamed like a new friend, one she could trust, a confidant to whom she could whisper her secrets.

"Such a good friend must have a name," Anne mused. "I'll call you Kitty."

Like most girls her age, Anne liked movie stars, cats, dogs, and boys. She liked to gobble down treats with her friends at the ice-cream parlor near her Amsterdam home in the Netherlands. She also loved to write. On June 12, 1942, she wrote her first entry in Kitty. The diary soon began to fill as Anne's thoughts burst across its pages as if they couldn't wait to be free.

One hot July afternoon, Anne put on her floppy hat, halter top, and plaid shorts. She stuffed her feet into sandals and climbed out onto the flat part of the roof of her house. She unfolded the canvas sling chair and scrunched up in it with a book. In the streets below, soldiers' heavy boots thudded past. Anne shuddered as she tried not to think about them, but it was hard to block their shadows from her mind.

Over the last two years as Amsterdam filled with German soldiers, her safe, familiar world had changed. Signs had appeared in shop windows, declaring, "Forbidden to Jews." Anne's family was Jewish. Some of her Jewish friends were scared to do anything these days. There were so many new rules for Jews that it made her head spin. Jews could not ride bicycles or use cars. They could only shop between three and five o'clock in the afternoon. Every Jew over six years old had to wear a big yellow star with "Jew" written on it so everyone would know who they were.

Hitler, the German leader, hated Jews. Anne wasn't sure why. People said he blamed the Jews for the poverty and high unemployment in Germany. That seemed ridiculous.

Sweat trickled from beneath her floppy hat, and she took it off to fan her face. As she tried to lose herself in the book, she heard the doorbell tinkle far below. Who could that be? Anne sat up straight, listening. After a few minutes, she heard footsteps thumping up the stairs. Her older sister, Margot, rushed onto the rooftop. Her cheeks burned with color.

"The S.S. have sent a call-up notice for Daddy!" she said.

Anne nearly dropped her book. Hitler's special troops, the S.S.! The Germans wanted to take their father away? Where would they take him? To one of those horrid concentration camps?

Anne hurried into the house, following her sister into their room. Margot collapsed onto the bed.

"Are you okay?" Anne knelt beside her, brushing a dark strand of hair from her forehead.

Margot shook her head. Tears glistened on the ends of her eyelashes.

"The notice isn't really for Daddy," she said. "It's for me."

Anne felt as if a hand had clamped over her mouth and nose, choking off her breath.

"Why?" she whispered. Margot was only 16. Why would the Germans want to take her away? They couldn't let that happen!

Anne's parents, Edith and Otto Frank, had no intention of allowing the Germans to take either of their daughters. For over a year, they'd been preparing for the time when they would have to go into hiding, though they'd hoped it would never come. They had stored food, clothes, and furniture—everything they would need—in secret rooms behind Mr. Frank's office building.

"Tomorrow we must go," Anne's mother warned.

Early the next morning, Anne's mother shook her awake.

"Dress now. Wear everything you can. We can't carry suitcases, or the Germans will become suspicious."

Anne layered on enough clothes for an Arctic trek. She pulled on two pairs of stockings, her summer shorts, and three pairs of pants. She topped these bulky clothes with a dress, a skirt, two vests, and a jacket. After wrapping a scarf around her neck, she perched a woolly cap atop her dark hair. She struggled to bend down to lace her shoes, feeling like an overstuffed doll; she could hardly breathe, much less move.

Wandering soundlessly through the house, Anne stared at the breakfast dishes cluttering the table. Her mother hadn't bothered to clear the dishes or make the beds. What was the point? Soon they would leave their home behind.

By the time they reached the office building, Anne's layers were soaked with rain. She felt like 20-pound sacks of potatoes were draped over her body. She could hardly wait to strip them off. The family scurried into the office building and up the stairs. Her father swung open a bookcase on a hidden door at the back of an office. Only a few people knew what waited behind that door: the Secret Annex.

Anne stared around her. The hidden rooms were even messier than the ones they'd left behind. All day long she cleaned, unpacked, filled cupboards, and made beds. When she finally had a free moment, she wandered upstairs into the tiny attic room. From one window, she could see a tall clock tower. From another, she spotted a large chestnut tree. She sighed. That's as close as I'll get to the outside for a long, long time, she thought.

For two long years, Anne only left the Secret Annex through the pages of her diary. Since she dreamed of becoming a writer, she kept a careful log of everything that happened. One day, she thought, she would use her diary to help her write a book. She would title it *The Secret Annex.*

 ## Comprehension Check

**1.** Why are there so many new rules for Jews in the Netherlands?

**2.** What is the significance of the diary in this story?

**3.** If you were in Anne's place, what would you do to fill the time while you were confined to the Secret Annex?

**4.** The Secret Annex was discovered by German soldiers. Anne and her sister, Margot, died in a German concentration camp. Her diary was found and published as *The Diary of Anne Frank.* Have you ever heard of Anne Frank? If so, what do you know about her and her family?

# Einstein's Dog

*by Kim T. Griswell*

I guess I should begin at the beginning, but who really knows where that is? It's all relative, you know. Anyway, my name is Chico, better known as Einstein's dog. So that means I'm no ordinary mutt. I may be small, but I've got big ideas floating between my ears, and Albert put them there.

If you didn't know better, you might take one look at Albert and think he's a raving lunatic. He has a head full of wild white hair that seems to defy the laws of gravity, but he's smarter than he looks. Of course, there was a time when even his parents thought he might be one bite short of a dog biscuit. Until he was nine years old, he couldn't speak fluently. He'd stop between sentences, as if he were rehearsing what he was going to say. Sometimes he'd start again.

And sports? They made his head spin. So while the other boys were out kicking balls and tackling one another, Albert was at home practicing his violin. He hated it at first, but once he discovered Mozart, he was hooked. I have to say that there's nothing I like more than curling up on my pillow in front of a crackling fire and being serenaded by Albert Einstein. It's a dog's life, as they say.

Now you're probably thinking that, being a genius and all, little Al was the perfect student. Ha! He was one of those kids who kept asking question after question. You know the ones.

"Who wrote *A Midsummer Night's Dream*?" your teacher might ask. Albert was the kind of kid who might raise his hand and say, "Well, sir, the play has been attributed to William Shakespeare, but I believe the evidence suggests that it might have been written by his sister."

And what is a teacher to say to that?

I'll tell you what his Greek teacher once said. "Your mere presence spoils the respect of the class for me."

"They were like lieutenants in the army, Chico," he told me. "They wanted my thoughts to march in rows—hup, two, three—like little soldiers! But my thoughts needed to wander about a bit before they landed on an idea."

I knew just what he was talking about. Catching an idea is kind of like chasing a butterfly. Just when you think one has landed and you are ready to pounce, it flits off again, heading for the next flower.

Anyway, Albert dropped out of school when he was 15, but he kept studying on his own. He had especially liked geometry in school. "I'll never forget my holy geometry book," he told me. I didn't know why a book with a hole in it was so special, until he said he meant the book was sacred, or very, very important to him. I guess what fascinated Albert was that the book taught him how to prove things logically. The rest is history.

Albert spent a lot of his time from then on doing research, trying to prove things. He proved that the visible motion of particles suspended in a liquid was due to the invisible motion of the molecules of the liquid. Who would have thought?

He even helped me understand how the radio worked when I couldn't get the little knob to tune to my favorite station.

"You see, the wire telegraph is a kind of a very, very long cat. You pull his tail in New York and his head is meowing in Los Angeles. Do you understand this?"

I growled softly. Anything that had to do with pulling a cat's tail, I could understand perfectly.

"Good," Albert continued. "Radio operates exactly the same way. You send signals here; they receive them there. The only difference is that there is no cat."

No cat? If there's no cat, then there's no tail to pull. Where's the fun in that?

I wandered back to my pillow. Sometimes I just didn't understand Albert at all. No cat!

Albert discovered the theory of relativity, you know, but I never quite understood it: $E = mc^2$, energy is equal to mass times the speed of light squared.

"Ah," he scratched me behind the ears, "there are harder things in the world to understand than that!"

I stuck out my tongue and panted, cocking my head to one side.

"Like what, you ask? Well, like the income tax. That, my dear Chico, is the hardest thing in the world to understand!

"Relativity is much simpler." He patted his lap to let me know it was okay to jump up there. After I got comfortable, he said, "It's like this. When you sit with a nice girl for two hours, it seems like two minutes. When you sit on a hot stove for two minutes, it seems like two hours. That's relativity."

Still, there's one thing I never could figure out. Why would Albert want to sit on a hot stove in the first place? Some genius!

Well, that's my story. You may think I'm just wagging your tail, but it's true.

## Comprehension Check

**1.** Who is telling this story?

**2.** To what does Albert Einstein compare the way a radio works?

**3.** Based on Chico's description, what do you think Albert was like?

**4.** What other stories have you read or heard that have been told from the point of view of a famous person's pet?

# Roald's Revenge

*by Kim T. Griswell*

I've heard people say that the books written by Roald Dahl take revenge on cruel adults who harm children. "Beastly people must be punished," Dahl once said. I had to find out for myself if this were true.

I gathered some of Dahl's books, such as *Matilda, The Magic Finger,* and *James and the Giant Peach.* I began reading, and sure enough, found that most of the adults in these books were mean and spiteful. But I wondered, how did Dahl come up with these story ideas, and did the cruel adults come from his own experiences? Then I read *Boy: Tales of Childhood.* What stories he had to tell in this one: some funny, some painful, but all true!

For instance, there was this one despicable old shopkeeper named Mrs. Pratchett. Every time the boys went into her sweetshop, she yelled at them as she reached her dirty, grubby hands into the jars of candy. In those days, there were few laws to force Mrs. Pratchett to wash her dirty fingernails or use a scoop to dig candies from a jar. After one too many stomachaches, the boys had to do something to get back at her. So who could blame them for what they would later call the great Mouse Plot?

Here's what happened. One day, Roald and his friends found a stinky dead mouse. Roald took that dead mouse to Mrs. Pratchett's shop. While she stuck her dirty hand into a box of Sherbet Suckers, he dropped the dead mouse into a jar of Gobstoppers. There it lay just waiting for Mrs. Pratchett to grab it.

Roald and his friends thought revenge was sweet until Mrs. Pratchett came down to the school and identified them as the guilty mouse plotters. The nasty whipping the headmaster gave Roald may have been enough to convince him that he had to find a safer way to get revenge. Perhaps that's why he decided to write books for children. He knew that children would appreciate the justice of a stinky dead mouse.

Maybe you think the great Mouse Plot took revenge too far. Perhaps a closer look at Roald's school days would help you understand his desire for fictional revenge. Roald attended an English boarding school for boys called a prep school. Through-out his school days, a number of unpleasant, painful things happened to him. He claimed that all of the stories were true, including the story of the pen nib.

What's a pen nib, you ask? During Roald's school days, students wrote with pens that had pointed tips called nibs. They had to dip the nibs into inkwells every few seconds as they wrote. Usually, pen nibs are harmless things. They hardly ever cause trouble. But when a pen nib tangles with an English prep school teacher, anything can happen.

The teachers in Roald's school were called masters. One mean and nasty master stood out from all the rest. His name was Captain Hardcastle. He had flaming red-orange hair and a bushy mustache that spread almost ear to ear.

Hardcastle seemed to have it in for Roald from the first day he walked into his class. He barked orders at Roald like an army captain, which he had been at one time.

"Pull your shoulders back!" Hardcastle commanded, his orange mustache flaring out with each word. "Get on with your work!"

Once during evening Prep, Roald hit his nib on the top of the desk and it broke. What was Roald to do? He knew that talking was forbidden and even raising his hand to ask a question could cause the wrath of Hardcastle. Desperate to finish, he broke the rule of silence.

He asked the boy beside him if he could borrow a nib. In an instant, Hardcastle exploded from the front of the room like a rocket, launching himself straight at

Roald.

"You're talking!" Hardcastle accused, his face turning as purple as a ripe turnip.

Roald tried to explain that he'd broken his nib and that he was only asking the other boy to lend him one, but Hardcastle wouldn't listen.

"You are lying!" Hardcastle's orange mustache twitched triumphantly, as if he'd just caught Roald in a plot to overthrow the headmaster and take possession of the school.

Roald was given a Stripe, which meant that he would be punished by the headmaster the next day. Roald must have been terrified.

The next morning, when Roald knocked on the headmaster's door, the headmaster had already heard Hardcastle's version of what happened. He did not want to hear anything Roald had to say. Slowly, he walked across his sitting room to a cupboard. He carefully chose a thin yellow cane and turned purposefully to face the trembling Roald.

"For talking in Prep," he said, "for trying to cheat and for lying, I am going to give you six strokes of the cane."

Can you believe that? If you were Roald Dahl, wouldn't you want revenge? Of course you would. It's only natural. But Roald was much nicer, and much more clever, than his tormentors. He wrote stories, wonderful fictional stories that allowed him to turn the tables on the cruel adults in his young life.

If you've read any of Roald Dahl's books, you know exactly what I'm talking about. If you haven't read his books, isn't it time you did?

 # Comprehension Check

**1.** What is the great Mouse Plot?

**2.** Why does Roald Dahl need to find a safer way to take revenge?

**3.** How do you think Roald Dahl gets revenge against "beastly people" by writing fiction?

**4.** Do you think it would be helpful to write about someone who has hurt you in some way? Why or why not?

# Top Dogs, Cats—and Goats?

*by Joanne Mattern*

"Why does everyone say 'It's a dog's life'? What's that supposed to mean anyway?"

Stumpy thumped his bobbed tail against the sidewalk and stared at the huge white house at the end of the curving drive.

"What do you mean, Stumpy?" asked his fluffball of a niece, Peaches.

"What I mean is that life can't be too tough for the pooches that live up there." The cat nodded toward the big house. "I'd trade the dog-eat-cat life we lead for the cushy life of a presidential pup any day."

Peaches stretched, fluffed out her white fur, and then padded across the White House lawn. Stumpy plodded along after her.

"It's like this," he said. "Every four years, people in the United States choose the person they want to be the country's president. No matter who is elected or what that person's politics are, one thing is for sure: The new president probably has a pet. Most United States presidents have had a pet, sometimes more than one. Over the past 200 years, the White House has been home to more than 400 cats and dogs."

"All at one time?" Peaches's gold-flecked eyes blinked in surprise.

"Of course not, silly. If a president had 400 cats and dogs, how would he ever get any work done?"

Peaches licked her whiskers and kept walking.

"The most common presidential pet is the dog," Stumpy said. "That's why I think dogs have it made. Presidents from George Washington to Bill Clinton have had a canine or two for company. In fact, Washington had 36 of them!"

"Did *he* get any work done?"

Stumpy's eyes looked toward the sky. "He was the father of our country. He must have gotten a few things done.

"Anyway, some White House dogs have been as famous as their owners. Franklin Delano Roosevelt had a Scottish terrier named Fala. Roosevelt trained Fala to stand on his hind legs when 'The Star-Spangled Banner' was played."

Peaches stopped to sharpen her claws on a tree trunk. "If I were a presidential pet, I wouldn't do any silly tricks. I would lounge on a red velvet cushion and eat caviar all day."

"Naw. That wouldn't be good." Stumpy scampered up a tree, perched on a limb, and peered down at Peaches. "You might get the president in trouble. Back in 1944, some people who didn't like Roosevelt claimed he spent $15,000 to send a Navy ship to bring Fala back from the Aleutian Islands. Roosevelt could have gotten into a lot of trouble, so I don't think the American people would be happy with a president spoiling his kitten with caviar!"

Peaches curled up near the tree in a pool of sunshine. Stumpy could almost see dreams of being a spoiled presidential pet floating over her head as she purred herself to sleep.

Stumpy remembered another famous presidential pooch, Checkers. Checkers belonged to Richard Nixon. He never lived in the White House, but if it weren't for him, Nixon might not have lived there either. In 1952, Nixon was running for vice president when he was accused of accepting money and gifts illegally. Nixon went on television and said that he had only accepted one gift—Checkers. Then he insisted that he was going to keep the dog because his children loved it so much. People enjoyed the speech enough that it probably helped save Nixon's political career. In 1969, he became president. While he was president, Nixon had an Irish setter named King Timahoe. He often introduced the dog to foreign leaders who came to the White House.

Stumpy stretched out on the tree branch, his thoughts of the former presidents swirling…. And what about Warren G. Harding? He had an Airedale named Laddie Boy. Laddie Boy attended meetings and even had his own chair. After Harding died in 1923, 19,000 newsboys contributed pennies to make a statue of the dog. Stumpy had seen the statue for himself when he snuck into the Smithsonian Institution to look at the national treasures.

Stumpy liked the statue of Laddie Boy. It couldn't chase him like most White House dogs. Things were always better when there was a cat in the White House. Why didn't people elect more cat lovers? There had been a cool cat in the house not long ago. The black-and-white cat arrived when President Bill Clinton moved in. Stumpy chuckled. Actually, President Clinton was allergic to cats. Socks the cat belonged to his daughter, Chelsea. He'd heard Socks even had his own Web page. Now that was one spoiled cat!

Cats and dogs were pretty ordinary pets for presidents. Stumpy had heard tales about really strange White House residents. Cows, sheep, an alligator, a goat, and a pony had all lived on the White House grounds. Some of them worked as hard as their owners while they were in office. President William Howard Taft's cow provided milk for the White House. President Woodrow Wilson raised sheep. He used their wool to make clothes and sheets for soldiers fighting in World War I.

Some of those strange pets caused trouble. Once, President Benjamin Harrison's goat ran away, and he had to chase the animal down the street. Stumpy would have loved to have seen that one. And how about the time Theodore Roosevelt's son, Archie, was sick in bed? Archie's brothers brought the family pony up to his room on the White House elevator!

That wasn't the worst of it. Calvin Coolidge owned a pair of raccoons, James Garfield kept a goat to pull his kids' sleigh, and John Quincy Adams let his alligator live in a White House bathtub!

Stumpy jumped down from the tree limb, right beside Peaches. She yowled to her feet.

"What did you do that for? I was dreaming about the soft, red cushion I'd be sleeping on if I lived in there." She pointed her pink nose toward the White House.

"Well," Stumpy said, "the next time a presidential election rolls around, maybe you should vote for a president who likes kittens."

"Silly," Peaches hissed. "Cats can't vote!"

## 🔖 Comprehension Check

**1.** What trick did President Roosevelt teach his dog Fala?

**2.** What is the main point of this story?

**3.** Which pet do you think was the most beneficial to its presidential master? Why?

**4.** Which presidential pet do you find the most interesting? Why?

# The Bone Hunter

*by Linda Sanders*

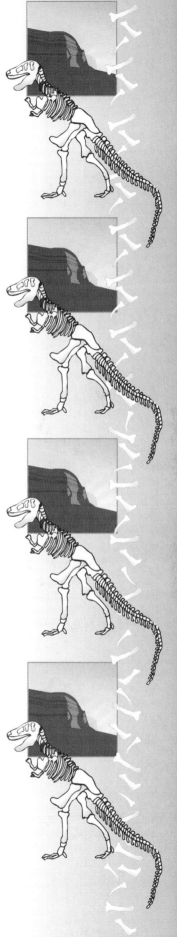

Sue Hendrickson watched impatiently as the August sun burned away the stubborn gray fog. She'd spent two hot, dusty months in the South Dakota Badlands. Now she had just two more days to find the treasure she had a feeling lay buried somewhere nearby.

Restlessly, she jumped up. She couldn't wait any longer. The rest of the team was in town getting the truck's flat tire repaired, but Sue seemed to hear the bluffs calling to her.

She strode over to her gear and swung on her pack. "Gypsy," she called. "Come!" The golden retriever bounded to her and the two headed off.

The steady hiking relaxed Sue's stiff muscles. The team had spent weeks kneeling under a blazing sun, carefully collecting chips from a triceratops skeleton. Everyone was exhausted, but Sue felt hopeful. She scanned the cliffs. She didn't bother with most of the bones she saw, so common they reminded her of popcorn bits littering the ground. She was after something rarer. "Today I'm going to find something special," she told herself.

Sue and Gypsy trudged on, putting miles between them and camp. Sue was heading for a sandstone bluff she'd noticed earlier. Something she couldn't explain—perhaps some slight difference in color or texture—drew her toward the hill.

The full heat of the day was bearing down by the time they reached it. Sue walked carefully, exploring each crack. The rock was from the Cretaceous period, the time when dinosaurs disappeared from the earth. The ground was scattered with pieces of bones—a good sign.

As she crept along, Sue noticed bone fragments that seemed to have fallen from a ledge overhead. She bent down for a better look. Then she drew in a sharp breath. The fragments were honeycombed, like a bird's bones. The time period of the rock and the texture of the bones could only mean the bones came from a large meat eater!

Her heart pounding, Sue stood up and studied the ledge. Just over her head, part of an enormous backbone poked out from the sandstone. Three bones lay together, just as they would have when the animal was alive. Sue stared in disbelief. She'd never found anything like these bones, but within moments she realized what they must be. She'd found the remains of a *Tyrannosaurus rex.*

Hardly daring to breathe, Sue chose a few fragments and packed them safely away. She whistled to Gypsy and started for camp. Her mind was spinning during the long walk. The chances of finding a *T. rex* were very slim—only 25 skeletons had ever been found—but this one seemed like it had been waiting for her.

As she neared camp, she broke into a run. She found Peter Larson, a fossil expert. Without saying much, she pulled out the bones and handed them to him.

Peter studied the fragments, then Sue's face. "Holy cow!" he screamed. "These are tyrannosaurus bones! How did you find them?"

As they hiked back, they could hardly contain their excitement. When they reached the site, they explored together. They found ribs and a thigh bone, and knew they had made a major discovery. Peter stepped back, put his hands on his hips, and looked at the scene. His eyes seemed to say, "This is the most wonderful thing we are ever going to dig."

Soon the whole team was working at the site. Slowly, the hard stone gave way and more bones were revealed: the animal's huge skull, its tail, legs, nearly all of its ribs, and, most unusual of all, one forelimb. After 17 days of back-breaking work, they had uncovered the largest and most complete *T. rex* skeleton ever found: almost 250 bones that added up to a dinosaur 13 feet high at the hips and 42 feet long.

It was the first step in a long process of studying and preparing the 67-million-year-old bones. Unveiled at Chicago's Field Museum of Natural History ten years later, it was the largest, most well-preserved, and complete skeleton ever discovered. Sue Hendrickson watched as the curtains fell, revealing the dinosaur towering on its giant hind legs with its powerful teeth bared. The world's most famous *T. rex* was now called Sue.

## Comprehension Check

**1.** Where is the rest of the fossil-finding team on the day Sue Hendrickson discovers the *T. rex* skeleton?

**2.** When Sue finds the bone fragments, how does she know they are unusual?

**3.** How do you think Sue and Peter feel about discovering the *T. rex* skeleton?

**4.** If you were a fossil finder like Sue Hendrickson, which extinct animal would you most want to find? Why?

# Anasazi: Ancient Ancestors

*by Rita Milios*

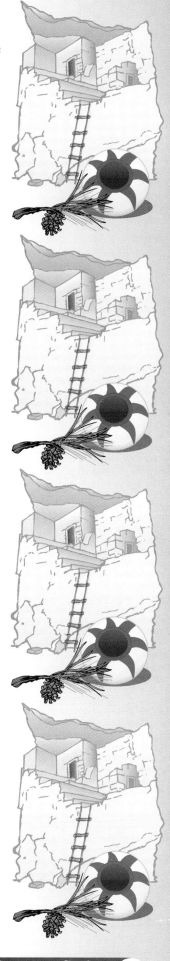

Picking gingerly among scrubby bushes, gravel, and stones, Adam and his grand-father paused in the chilly morning air to watch the sun rise above the flat-topped mountain called Mesa Verde.

"Look, Grandson. You can see far from here," said the spry, elderly man with the weathered, wrinkled face. "This is the place we call four corners. Here New Mexico, Arizona, and Utah meet our state of Colorado. And here we will find the spirits of our ancestors, the ancient ones, the ones we call Anasazi."

The old man closed his eyes, took a deep breath, and exhaled slowly. "It still feels like home," he said. "Come, I will show you."

Adam shivered and reluctantly followed. Sometimes, he thought his grandfather went a little too far with his Native American folklore. Adam would much rather have been at home in his comfortable, warm bed this early in the morning. Instead, he scrambled after his grandfather, exploring the ruins of an ancient civilization. The natives had lived here on the green mesa. When the Spanish saw the flat-topped mountain in 1770, they called it *Mesa Verde,* which means "green table" in Spanish.

Thirteen-year-old Adam had never been to Mesa Verde. It was the home of many ancient Anasazi ruins left by the tribes who had first lived on the top of the mesa and who had later cut their village homes directly into the sides of the steep mountain cliffs. Little was known about these mysterious people believed to be Native American ancestors, except for the telltale signs of their civilization. Ruins were discovered in 1888 by two cowboys. Clay and stone houses fit neatly into narrow canyon crevices, and single rooms called *kivas* were found cut into the hard, packed ground.

Coming to the edge of a cliff, Adam looked down and gasped. "Whoa!" he said. "Look at that!"

His grandfather chuckled softly. "Possibly up to 200 people lived together in that little village," he said. "They farmed here on the mesa top and then they may have carried their harvest to those cliffs in clay pots and baskets they had made. Here," he said, picking up a small pinecone. "This was one of their food sources. They also used the needles of the pine tree as medicine. The Anasazi were very resourceful."

"Can we go down there?" asked Adam, suddenly interested in his family history.

"Of course," said his grandfather with a grin.

"Did our ancestors, the ancient ones, eat these, too?" Adam pointed to some wild berries.

"They may have," his grandfather answered. "I'm sure they ate every food available to them. As their population grew, they found it harder and harder to feed everyone. Perhaps that's one reason they moved to the cliffs after nearly 700 years on the mesa top. They needed all the land they had to grow food. Then, after about 100 years, in the late 1200s, they left the mesa forever."

"That's too bad," said Adam. "What kind of crops did they grow?"

"Many of the foods you still eat today, Grandson. Corn, beans, and squash. Ah, here we are now."

"A ladder!"

"Yes, very much like the ones your ancestors used. Go ahead!"

Adam quickly scurried down the ladder and peered into the entrance of the rectangular stone and clay building. He ran his hand across the rough, cool stones. For a moment, he could almost smell smoke from a fire and the scent of roasting corn. He tried to imagine himself living here, sleeping by the hearth, perhaps on a mat of twigs and grass. He walked over to the ceremonial kiva and looked down into its deep pit,

picturing a fire there and people worshiping or socializing.

"Why did they leave here, Grandfather?" Adam asked, suddenly aware that this difficult but simple life would probably have had something very special to offer— community spirit and goodwill.

"Some say they were overtaken by warring tribes, but there's little evidence. Most believe they simply ran out of food following several years of drought and moved on."

"But they left something behind."

"Oh, yes. There's plenty of pottery and tools in the museums."

"No, Grandfather. I meant you and me. The ancient ones left us, their descendants, in the four corners. And they left their spirits to move through us."

## Comprehension Check

**1.** Why doesn't Adam want to explore the Anasazi ruins at the beginning of the story?

**2.** What relation are the Anasazi to Adam and his grandfather?

**3.** Why do you think Adam becomes interested in his family history?

**4.** Who are your ancestors and where did they live?

# Row, Maggie, Row!

*by Kim T. Griswell*

The ship was luxurious, with tennis courts, Turkish baths, elevators, and a gymnasium. Some of the wealthiest people in the world dined in its charming Café Parisien and relaxed in the first-class lounge modeled after the Palace of Versailles. Beneath an ornate domed skylight of glass and wrought iron, a curved, polished oak staircase led toward the first-class reception room. The staterooms in first-class were also very elegant.

On the night of April 14, 1912, Maggie Brown reclined atop the brass bed in her stateroom, trying to finish a book before she dozed off. Though she was wealthy—she'd paid a hefty $4,350 for her passage—she wasn't born with a silver spoon in her mouth. Her first taste of wealth came when her husband, J. J. Brown, discovered one of the largest silver mines in the United States. Overnight, Maggie, the daughter of an Irish immigrant ditchdigger, became a wealthy young woman who wanted nothing more than to be accepted into society.

Though she spent more time and money on becoming civilized than most, Maggie's tough, loud-talking ways couldn't be polished as easily as silver. She bought a mansion, attended the opera, and threw lavish parties, but none of that could take the hard edge off Maggie Brown. Though her hard-working past did not make her the most popular woman on board, it gave her qualities that would stand her in good stead as the night wore on.

Close to midnight, something crashed into the window above Maggie's head, throwing her onto the floor. She picked herself up and headed into the hall to find out what had happened. Men in pajamas swarmed into the gangway. Along with Maggie, they listened, trying to decide whether anything serious had happened. It was strangely quiet. Maggie could feel no movement underfoot, as if the ship's engines had ground to a stop.

No one seemed alarmed. After all, they had an experienced captain aboard, Edward J. Smith, known as the Millionaire's Captain. He'd never been wrecked, or, he claimed, in any situation that threatened to end in disaster. Smith would be retiring after this voyage, having logged over two million miles on White Star liners.

The huge ship was as big a celebrity as its captain; it was built to be unsinkable. So when the order came for the passengers to come up on deck with their life belts on, Maggie wasn't worried. If worse came to worse, she could swim.

Even beneath the furs she'd pulled on before going on deck, Maggie could feel the ice chilling the sea around them. Steam screamed from the boilers as crew members tried to ease the pressure building in them. Nearby, the captain directed crew members to ready the 16 wooden lifeboats and the four collapsible boats. Maggie soon learned that the unsinkable ship had hit an iceberg and was going down by the bow.

"Permission to begin loading, sir!" Officer Lightoller shouted to the captain.

Captain Smith nodded his agreement. Someone nearby grabbed hold of Maggie.

"You are going too," a deep voice said.

Before she could say yes or no, Maggie found herself dropped four feet into lifeboat No. 6. She found a seat among the women on board. The ship's quartermaster, Robert Hitchens, shivered from far more than the cold.

"There's only one seaman on that boat!" someone yelled.

Major Godfrey Peuchen, the vice commander of the Royal Canadian Yacht

Club, stood nearby.

"I'll go," he volunteered.

He swung himself down into the boat, which Maggie saw now held about 28 passengers. Peuchen and Hitchens were the only males.

As the lifeboat bumped into the black sea, Peuchen turned to Hitchens.

"Give one of the women the tiller so you can do some rowing," he said.

Hitchens burst out in a frightened voice, "There's no point in rowing. *Titanic*'s so large, she'll take everything for miles around down with her when she goes."

His eyes were wild with fright. "And if we escape the suction, the boilers will burst and rip up the bottom of the sea. It'll tear the icebergs asunder and completely submerge us."

Maggie glared at him. What was he doing? Trying to scare them to death?

"If you don't want to row, we will," she said. "It'll keep us warm!"

"Madam, that is out of the question," Hitchens said.

"What's out of the question is that we sit here and sink," said Maggie. "Now get out of the way or I'll throw you overboard!"

Maggie had learned to steer a boat on the Mississippi River as a young girl, and she certainly wasn't afraid of hard work. With the help of the other women, she pulled the boat away from the ship. Rowing soon warmed her, but some of the women could not stop shivering. Starting with her furs, Maggie peeled off layers of clothing and shared them with the other women.

The sights and sounds of that night would haunt Maggie and the other survivors for the rest of their lives. The lifeboats would not hold all of the passengers. As the ship sank into the glass-black sea, passengers prayed aloud and wept.

Maggie rowed the sluggish lifeboat through rough seas that were surrounded by huge icebergs for nearly seven and a half hours. Slowly, she made her way toward the *Carpathia*, a ship that had steamed through the night in response to the *Titanic*'s plea for help. Tired as she was, her hardy, working-class background wouldn't let her stop even after she was safely aboard. She bustled about nursing survivors, practicing the foreign languages she could speak to aid immigrant passengers, and raising funds to be used later for destitute victims. By the time the *Carpathia* steamed into New York City, Maggie already had pledges of $10,000.

Reporters gathered around her at the dock.

"Mrs. Brown?" one asked. "How did you manage to survive?"

Maggie paused for a moment, then she grinned. "Typical Brown luck," she said. "We're unsinkable."

---

##  Comprehension Check

**1.** What first happens to alert Maggie that something has gone wrong with the ship?

**2.** Why did Maggie take control of rowing the lifeboat?

**3.** Why do you think Maggie continues to help the victims after the sinking?

**4.** What qualities do you think make Maggie unsinkable?

# Answer Keys

**Page 7**
1. Dave is protective of the tomatoes because he grew them himself.
2. Students' answers will vary. One possible response: Dave feels sad about moving because he doesn't want to leave behind the house he's always lived in and all of his friends.
3. This story is funny because Frank thinks Dave has worms in his box, which makes him think that Dave eats worms.
4. Allow for discussion.

**Page 9**
1. Cody thinks spending an afternoon at the arcade without his little sister would be better.
2. Cody wants to trade his tickets for a stuffed basset hound because it looks like the dog he had to give away when he moved.
3. Students' responses will vary. One possible response: Emily probably loves her brother because she traded her tickets to get the stuffed basset hound for him.
4. Students' responses will vary. One possible response: The stuffed basset hound will help Cody get over having to give away his dog because it will help him remember George.

**Page 11**
1. Jill is in detention because her bike had a flat tire, making her late to school.
2. If Mrs. Nelson catches a student talking during detention, the student gets two hours of detention the next afternoon.
3. Allow for discussion.
4. Students' responses will vary. One possible response: The mouse probably runs toward Mrs. Nelson because it is trying to get away from the loud screaming.

**Page 13**
1. Nestor connects limestone to limes and lemons, which are citrus fruits. Because limes are green, he also thinks of Ireland and shamrocks. Nestor connects wolframite to wolfhounds. He connects serpentine to serpents, or snakes.
2. Mr. Bezelbaum is trying to teach his class about different types of rocks.
3. Mr. Bezelbaum doesn't like Nestor's comments. In the story, he tries to ignore Nestor when he raises his hand. He scrunches up his mouth. He asks, "Do I dare?" before picking up another rock. He dares Nestor with his eyes not to come up with another silly answer. He sighs.
4. Students' responses will vary. One possible response: Yes. During the story, she seems like a serious student who wouldn't make jokes like Nestor does.

**Page 15**
1. The brothers are the only ones in the movie theater because it's very late and the movie isn't any good.
2. Trevor and Darnel are sleepy during the movie because it's after midnight and they've eaten a lot of junk food.
3. Students' responses will vary. One possible response: They could have been having the same nightmare because they are so much alike.
4. Students' responses will vary. One possible response: The boys' mom probably won't let them go to another midnight movie because all they did was eat junk food and fall asleep.

**Page 17**
1. Hannah seems weird to the other students because of the way she dresses.
2. Based on clues from the story, *articulate* means "having a way with words and knowing how to use them."
3. Hannah turns the tables on the teasers by using knock-knock jokes to tease them back.
4. Allow for discussion.

**Page 19**
1. Gina's mother pays close attention to details because she is an editor.
2. Gina doesn't want to wear her helmet because it messes up her hair.
3. Gina changes her mind because she discovers how hard the wind is blowing on the beach when she is almost blown off her feet and sand scratches her eyes.
4. Allow for discussion.

**Page 21**
1. Jimmy keeps a close watch on the trail because he is looking for signs of grizzly bears.
2. Jimmy thinks Rob has no respect for his elders.
3. Based on information from the story, Jimmy probably comes from a Native American culture because of his name.
4. Students' responses will vary. One possible response: Before hiking in grizzly country, you should talk to park rangers to find out how to protect yourself.

**Page 23**
1. Monroe doesn't bring any water with him on the desert hike. He wears canvas sneakers instead of boots. He goes behind a boulder into a shaded area where snakes might hide.
2. Monroe thinks Victor would not be aware of the dangers in Los Angeles just as he is not aware of the dangers in the desert.
3. Victor knows a lot about the desert and the kinds of snakes that are found there. He knows that there are rattlesnakes in the desert. He also recognizes the hognose snake when he sees it.
4. Students' responses will vary. One possible response: Victor lives in the desert and knows a lot about the outdoors. He likes to hike. Monroe lives in the city. He probably likes to play video games, go to the mall, or skateboard.

**Page 25**
1. Cyrus is surprised because his dad got him pajamas the year before, even though he'd asked for a moped.
2. Cyrus doesn't want to skate down Meyer's Hill because he just got his skateboard and the hill is dangerous.
3. Students' responses will vary. One possible response: Murphy doesn't really want to skate down the hill. He hesitates at the top, just like Cyrus does. He's sweating, as if he's nervous. And when the kids run away, he offers to teach Cyrus to skate on level ground instead of racing down the hill.
4. At the beginning of the story, Cyrus thinks that Murphy is the meanest, toughest shark of a skateboarder. At the end of the story, Murphy is more friendly, so Cyrus probably changes his mind about Murphy.

**Page 27**
1. Mary wants to chase the storm because she wants to be a meteorologist as soon as she finishes college.
2. Mary tells Jimmi that Ben Franklin was a storm chaser. Jimmi says that just because one of the founding fathers chased storms doesn't mean they have to.
3. After reading about tornado safety, Jimmi scouts the area to make sure he knows where all the safe places are.
4. Allow for discussion.

**Page 29**
1. The main character doesn't want to go to Florida for Christmas because there won't be any snow and she doesn't think she can find the magic of Christmas in Florida.
2. To make Florida seem more Christmasy, Edward shows her how to make angels in the sandbox and sled down the hill on a skateboard.
3. Students' responses will vary. One possible response: Edward probably doesn't like entertaining his cousin because she keeps complaining and he tells her to stop whining.
4. Allow for discussion.

## Page 31

1. Hogan doesn't usually catch any fish because he's too noisy and he doesn't have any patience.
2. The heron walks slowly and stealthily, while the gulls and cormorants dive down from the air and catch fish.
3. Fishing requires stillness because noise frightens the fish away. It requires patience because a fisherman may need to keep his line in one place for a long time in order to get a bite.
4. Allow for discussion.

## Page 33

1. Lionel doesn't want to drive the sub crazy because she is his new stepmother.
2. Students' responses will vary. One possible response: Lionel resents her because he says that he didn't ask for a stepmother.
3. Students' responses will vary. One possible response: Lionel would not have put the snake in the drawer because he knows his stepmother is afraid of snakes and he remembers the cookies she had made.
4. Allow for discussion.

## Page 35

1. The vote for class president has to be recounted because the teacher found five more votes that had fallen behind her desk, and Morgan had won by only a small margin.
2. Students' responses will vary. One possible response: They don't trust each other. Kevin accuses Morgan of cheating. Morgan tells Nancy to keep an eye on Kevin and Bob when she leaves the room, so she must not trust them to win fairly.
3. Morgan knows that something is wrong with the second count because Kevin won by six votes. When the votes were counted previously, Morgan had won by four. Even if Kevin got all five of the new votes, he would have won by only one vote.
4. Allow for discussion.

## Page 37

1. Casey is nervous about the recital because it is her first one.
2. Students' responses will vary. One possible response: Casey probably feels embarrassed and angry at herself.
3. Roger probably means that it took a lot of nerve for Casey to go back out onstage.
4. Allow for discussion.

## Page 39

1. Kendall is working hard over the summer break because he wants to buy his mother something special for her birthday.
2. Students' responses will vary. One possible response: Kendall loves his mom.
3. Students' responses will vary. One possible response: Kendall will be able to earn the money because he has done it before.
4. Allow for discussion.

## Page 42

1. *Tidal wave* is another name for tsunami.
2. Owen's father goes into town because he is the sheriff. He has to help everyone get to safety.
3. Owen is courageous and can keep a cool head in a dangerous situation.
4. Allow for discussion.

## Page 44

1. Winny's favorite detective is Sherlock Holmes.
2. The students are probably excited about the special guest because he makes chocolate.
3. When Winny finds that none of the students bit into the chocolate, wheels squeaking in the hallway remind her that Mr. Tidy was also in their room. She remembers that he was the last one to leave the room when they went out to recess.
4. Allow for discussion.

## Page 47

1. The lighthouse keeper thinks the ghost of Captain DeWolf haunts the lighthouse because of the following: she's encountered what she believes to be a ghost every day since coming to live in the lighthouse, the captain's ship sank near the lighthouse, and unexplained fingerprints are found on his belongings.
2. The lighthouse keeper probably thinks that greed sank the *Brother Jonathan* because Captain DeWolf asked the company's agent to stop taking on cargo, but he refused.
3. The *Brother Jonathan* could have sunk because it was overloaded with more freight than it was designed to carry. Also, Captain DeWolf tried to bring his ship back to the harbor, but his map wasn't accurate and the ship crashed on a rock.
4. Students' responses will vary. One possible response: Captain DeWolf might have continued to sail out to sea rather than turn back.

## Page 49

1. Chloe might encounter a flash flood because it has been raining for three days, the weatherman says it's still raining on Grandfather Mountain, there is a flash flood warning in effect, and she hears something that sounds like water running in a toilet.
2. If Chloe rode into the water, she probably would have been swept off her bike.
3. Chloe saves Ms. Calihan by tying the rope she has in her pack to a tree. Then she ties a video to the other end of the rope so she can throw it to the librarian.
4. Students' responses will vary. One possible response: Chloe will not have to pay for the video. Ms. Calihan might pay for it because Chloe saved her.

## Page 51

1. Laura thinks they will find a treasure in the boarded-up mansion because stories passed down through their family tell of a hidden treasure there.
2. Students' responses will vary. One possible response: Meg probably believes that Union soldiers ransacked the house because they were known to have ransacked Southern homes during the Civil War.
3. Allow for discussion.
4. Allow for discussion.

## Page 53

1. You can tell that this story takes place in the future because it says that the last big earthquake in San Francisco took place in 1906, 148 years earlier. You can also tell because we don't have medibots that can heal broken legs.
2. Paco's mother works for Nanintech, a company that builds nanobots.
3. Paco decides to use the medibots to heal his broken leg because he can't help Mrs. Wilkins out of the damaged apartment with a broken leg. He thinks they should get out of the apartment because of aftershocks and the possibility of explosions and fires caused by the leaking gas.
4. Allow for discussion.

## Page 55

1. This race is unusual because it has a real dog racing against a robot dog.
2. This race seeks to prove which is better: something alive, such as a real dog, or something man-made, such as a robot dog.
3. Buddy wins the race because Robo trips over a rock, does a flip, and lands on his back.
4. Students' responses will vary. One possible response: Ben probably feels that a robot sister would be less trouble than a real sister. Using the remote control, he could control his robot sister and get her to do whatever he wanted her to do.

**Page 58**
1. Jamil's neighborhood is getting run-down and dangerous.
2. Jamil's aunt gives him the advice she does because she wants to encourage him. She wants him to realize that he can get out of his dying neighborhood if he tries hard enough.
3. Students' responses will vary. One possible response: Zeke is probably telling Jamil that one of the animals will take him somewhere he needs to go in order to learn a lesson.
4. Allow for discussion.

**Page 60**
1. Travis thinks Gramps is crazy because he believes that dinosaurs did not become extinct. He thinks they left Earth in spaceships and went to live on another planet.
2. Gramps is talking about the theory that the dinosaurs became extinct when an asteroid hit the earth.
3. Travis's grandfather has really left him in charge of a dinosaur egg.
4. Allow for discussion.

**Page 62**
1. The box is special to Gideon because his mother gave it to him just before she died.
2. The phrase "all that glitters is not gold" means that there are good things in life that have nothing to do with money.
3. Students' responses will vary. One possible response: Lucia is probably not happy. She seems sad because her father is too busy to spend time with her.
4. Allow for discussion.

**Page 64**
1. Scott is sleeping outside the tent because inside the tent it's crowded and smelly and his father snores.
2. Scott's family is camping in a western desert.
3. Students' responses will vary. One possible response: Scott and the small blue alien probably keep it a secret because they want to protect one another.
4. Allow for discussion.

**Page 66**
1. This story takes place on a planet called Exodus, which orbits around Alpha Centauri, a star 4.35 light-years from Earth.
2. Players bounce a two-inch ball down the court on elbows, knees, or heads. They score by using a racket to smash the ball past the other team's defense into the hot pink electronic buzzer set in the wall behind the goal line. Only smashers can turn off their antigravity devices during play.
3. Students' responses will vary. One possible response: Studying the schematics helps Xijohn win the game because otherwise he wouldn't have known that his final play is legal.
4. Allow for discussion.

**Page 68**
1. Mari first discovers her horse's talent for dancing when she plays a Louis Armstrong CD while mucking out his stall and he starts to prance from side to side.
2. Mari's father doesn't want anyone to know that Sybaris can dance because the other racehorse trainers will laugh at him. They won't take his horse seriously as a racer.
3. Students' responses will vary. One possible response: Jason isn't very nice because he makes fun of Sybaris, and then he cheats to try to help his horse win the race.
4. Students' responses will vary. One possible response: Mari might keep quiet about what happened because she won't want her father to know what happened. He won't let Sybaris dance anymore if he finds out.

**Page 70**
1. At first, David's parents won't let him have a pet because he's too young. Later, they say that pets are too messy, their apartment is too small, and they can't afford to feed a pet.
2. David feels disappointed. He wants a real pet that he can play with.
3. David solves his pet problem by convincing his neighbor, Mrs. Palmer, to share a kitten with him.
4. Allow for discussion.

**Page 72**
1. Sara and Jessie identify Hairy by looking in Sara's *Field Guide to Spiders*. They match Hairy's size, coloring, and markings to a spider in the book.
2. Sara's mother is probably afraid of spiders because she shudders when Sara tells her about the spider and she plans to kill him.
3. Jessie probably feels the same way Sara does because Jessie seems to like spiders and she doesn't act afraid when Sara shows Hairy to her.
4. Allow for discussion.

**Page 74**
1. Maria is taking an imaginary journey, pretending to be a pelican.
2. A pelican folds its wings and dives into the water with enough force to stun fish beneath it. Then it uses its throat pouch as a net to scoop up the stunned fish.
3. Allow for discussion.
4. Allow for discussion.

**Page 76**
1. Her mother thinks that animals are dumb.
2. Amanda's morning job is to sweep the chapel and light the candles.
3. It is apparent that an earthquake occurs because the chapel rocks and then rumbles, knocking Amanda off her feet and the candles off their silver sticks, and the floor pitches like the deck of a rolling ship.
4. Allow for discussion.

**Page 78**
1. This story takes place in the dunes along the beach near Coos Bay, Oregon.
2. Students' responses will vary. One possible response: The black mare heads for freedom because she doesn't like to be penned up.
3. The author describes the mare as being almost all black, having a flowing mane, having a tail that brushes the ground, standing over 15 hands tall, and having a small white star on her forehead.
4. Allow for discussion.

**Page 80**
1. At the beginning of the story, John listens to the news about Mount St. Helens to find out if it is going to erupt.
2. The Great Spirit turns the two chiefs into mountains because they are causing too much destruction to the earth. He turns Loowit into a mountain because he does not want to turn her back into an old witch and she no longer wants to be a beautiful young woman.
3. Students' responses will vary. One possible response: Native Americans probably made up tales to try to explain things they didn't understand, such as volcanic eruptions.
4. Allow for discussion.

**Page 82**
1. Shing creates the best designs, Jun cuts the best patterns, and Lei sews the finest stitches.
2. The three brothers decide to make separate gowns because they become greedy; each wants the gold for himself.
3. The brothers learn that they will be stronger if they work together.
4. Allow for discussion.

**Page 84**

1. Ashi wishes to be something else because he thinks that he is the most powerless of creatures.
2. Ashi becomes a rich man, a king, the sun, a cloud, and a rock.
3. Ashi is never satisfied because he always finds something else that is more powerful than he is.
4. Allow for discussion.

**Page 86**

1. The two brothers journey beyond the village to hunt goats in the mountains.
2. Raven gives the boys a bundle of sticks, a small bag of stones, a skin bag filled with water, and a skin bag filled with oil. The sticks grow into trees, the stones grow into hills and mountains, and the water becomes rivers and lakes, all of which temporarily bar the giant's path. The oil gets in the giant's eyes, which allows the elder brother to slip out of his hands; then Raven touches the oil with a feather and the giant turns into smoke and ash.
3. Students' responses will vary. One possible response: The Tlingit probably made up stories because they wanted to make sense of the world around them.
4. Allow for discussion.

**Page 88**

1. Margaret and Patrick travel to America because they are looking for better opportunities.
2. Margaret decides not to take off her coat and leave the roped-off area because her brother has told her to trust her new country.
3. Students' responses will vary. (The *P* actually meant that further medical inspection was needed for "physical and lungs.")
4. Allow for discussion.

**Page 90**

1. When Masey lights the birthday candle and wishes Ben a happy birthday, the statue of Ben Franklin comes to life.
2. Masey loves to read and so did Ben.
3. When Masey says that Ben has written things worth reading, she's referring to the Declaration of Independence. When she says he has done things worth writing about, she is referring to his many inventions and discoveries.
4. Allow for discussion.

**Page 92**

1. Hendrik needs to earn money to help Grootpapa pay the money he owes for the windmill they live in.
2. People are willing to trade sacks of wheat, pounds of cheese, pigs, a silver cup, a bed with bedding, bushels of rye, and sheep.
3. Students' responses will vary. One possible response: The people bidding on Hendrik's tulip bulb are probably hoping it will be a very valuable bulb.
4. Allow for discussion.

**Page 94**

1. Mr. Ford is worried because automobile sales are down. Because of the depression, farmers can't sell their crops; therefore, they can't afford to buy cars.
2. Jasper suggests that Mr. Ford find a way to use soybeans in automobile manufacturing because if the farmers sell Mr. Ford the soybeans they grow, then they'll be able to afford to buy cars again.
3. Allow for discussion.
4. Students' responses will vary. The correct response: Mr. Ford knew that "If we want the farmer to be our customer, we must find a way to be his." So his chemists began researching to find products that could be made from plants.

**Page 96**

1. There are so many new rules for Jews in the Netherlands because German soldiers are now in the country and their leader, Hitler, hates Jews.
2. The diary becomes Anne's confidant, her friend, and her way to escape her confinement in the Secret Annex.
3. Allow for discussion.
4. Allow for discussion.

**Page 98**

1. Chico, Albert Einstein's dog, is telling this story.
2. Einstein compares the way a radio works to pulling a cat's tail in New York, making it meow in Los Angeles.
3. Students' responses will vary. One possible response: Based on Chico's description, Albert Einstein was very smart and kind of strange. He wasn't a very good student in school and gave his teachers a lot of trouble.
4. Allow for discussion.

**Page 100**

1. The great Mouse Plot is a plot by Roald Dahl and his friends to get back at Mrs. Pratchett, a mean, dirty woman they don't like. They find a dead mouse, and Roald puts it in a jar of Gobstoppers so that she'll grab it when she reaches into the jar.
2. Roald Dahl needs to find a safer way to take revenge because the headmaster of his school gives him a beating when he gets caught taking revenge against Mrs. Pratchett.
3. Students' responses will vary. One possible response: Roald Dahl gets revenge against "beastly people" when he writes fiction by creating characters that are like them and then having those characters get what they deserve in the end.
4. Allow for discussion.

**Page 102**

1. President Roosevelt taught Fala to stand on his hind legs when "The Star-Spangled Banner" was played.
2. The main point of this story is that many presidents have had pets.
3. Allow for discussion.
4. Allow for discussion.

**Page 104**

1. On the day Sue Hendrickson discovers the *T. rex* skeleton, the rest of the fossil-finding team is in town getting the truck's flat tire repaired.
2. Sue knows the bone fragments are unusual because they are honeycombed, like a bird's bones, and their texture tells her that they came from a large meat eater.
3. Students' responses will vary. One possible response: Sue and Peter are very excited because they probably believe this is the most important discovery they'll ever make.
4. Allow for discussion.

**Page 106**

1. Adam doesn't want to explore the Anasazi ruins at the beginning of the story because it's very early in the morning. He's cold and he'd rather be at home in bed.
2. Adam and his grandfather may be descendants of the Anasazi.
3. Students' responses will vary. One possible response: Adam becomes interested in his family history because he thinks the ruins are cool once he sees them.
4. Allow for discussion.

**Page 108**

1. Maggie is alerted that something has gone wrong with the ship when something crashes into the window, throwing her onto the floor of her stateroom.
2. Maggie takes control of rowing the lifeboat in order to keep the women from being scared and to warm them up.
3. Students' responses will vary. One possible response: Maggie probably continues to help the disaster victims after the sinking because she feels sorry for the ones who have lost so much.
4. Students' responses will vary. One possible response: Maggie is unsinkable because she is used to working hard and she doesn't give up when things get tough.